# DREAM
## GIVER

❖ COURSE WORKBOOK ❖

# BRUCE
# WILKINSON

 Prepare yourself! We're about to take a look inside your heart. And what do I know about hearts? I know one thing: that every one of them is the home of a wonderful dream. Everywhere I have traveled, I've listened to people share a common theme: *I have a dream.*

But a sad disclaimer is too often attached: *I don't know how to get there.* This is a world filled with dreamers, because it is owned by the Dream Giver. But what's exciting is knowing that the Dream Giver would never whisper a destination without providing a road map. Those dreams are meant to be achieved—and why not now?

I challenge you to look into your heart and take hold of your dream. Then we'll look to the One who created both hearts and dreams. What we find cannot fail to change us forever.

Shall we dream on?

*Bruce Wilkinson*

Project Director and Designer: Dorit Radandt; Writers: Rob Suggs and William Kruidenier

# TABLE
## *of* CONTENTS

## Pursuing Your Dream

When Disney World held its grand opening in Orlando, Florida, the widow of Walt Disney attended the ceremony. The great park was beautiful, exceeding every hope and dream. Someone walked up to Mrs. Disney and said, "I wish Walt could have seen this." She smiled and replied, "He did." If there hadn't been a Walt Disney to dream it into existence, Disney World would never have been built.

Take a walk through the world of today and look closely. All that you see, all that you hear, is a result of some individual's passionate dream. Many thought the "horseless carriage" would never make it, but there was one dreamer who closed his eyes and saw streets filled with automobiles. A top computing executive once remarked that the average home had no use for a computer; but someone else had a dream that compelled him to disprove that preconception.

Each new change in our world comes to pass because someone gazes into the realm of possibility rather than of mere actuality. Dreams are amazing seeds; they sprout into new wonders that change the world forever.

That's fine, you might remark, for pioneers and saints and inventors. But what about the rest of us?

The fact is, you, too, are a dreamer. Every stride you have taken—in education, in family, in vocation—has been propelled by the high-energy fuel of your dreams and visions. But those were only the beginning. Even now, there is the seed of a dream within you. Will you help it grow?

> *Reach high, for stars lie hidden in your soul.*
> *Dream deep, for every dream precedes the goal.*
> —Pamela Vaull Starr

> *Dreams grab us and move us. They are capable of lifting us to new heights and overcoming self-imposed limitations.*
> —Robert Kriegel

Some of us are skeptical about whether every human being is a dreamer. Perhaps we doubt because we see so few people pursuing their dreams. But try to imagine a life with no dream to captivate it. What would that be like? It would be a life without hope, purpose, or motivation. The dreamless soul would be little more than an organism, eating and sleeping, filling out its day between the womb and the tomb.

Dreams are what set us apart as God's children. He gave us our personalities, our gifts, our own fingerprints, and our own dreams. They are fragile and precious, like candles illuminating our souls within. Their brightness reveals a snapshot of the world we would most dearly want to inhabit. They reveal the activity we would choose above all others in life. They set out the goal we instinctively feel we were made to pursue.

What would we trade simply for the experience of the quest of this dream? Nearly everything! Where would we go in order to see it to fruition? Nearly anywhere! What would we give in price? All our lives, all our time; everything we have to give. It would be like the precious pearl described by Jesus; one would give away all that he owns just to possess it.

Nothing within us is more powerful than the dream, except the Lord who placed it there and gave it His power. He knitted its delicate threads into the very fabric of your soul. It is essentially who you are, and your imagination will eventually take its very shape.

How, then, can you follow your dream?

First we must ask: What if it is impossible? Many people quickly state that this is so. "I cannot follow my dream because _____." With what reason would you fill in that blank? Finances? Family? Timing? Abilities? A little reflection would show you that they are not truly reasons at all. Is there no way in all the world to raise those finances? Would your family really prevent you? Is the timing really impossible?

Your feelings toward the dream really hinge upon your feelings toward God, don't they? After all, He made every ounce of you. Would the God you love fasten your soul to a dead-end dream? Would He assign you a journey without a road?

And above all, is anything really impossible if God wants it done?

These are important questions! Answer them carefully, for your responses will reroute your dream and your life.

This is a course about a God who is, among other things, a Dream Giver and a Dream Enabler. He is not concerned with fear and limitations, but with joy and possibility. He wants you to chase that dream even more than you yourself want it, because He knows that all roads lead back to Him. In the end, He is the dream—and His dream is you. He is the destination, the first step, and the journey's end for the one great adventure your life has always awaited.

So bring your dream and your heart. It's time for that adventure to unfold.

> *I have been going through the process of reevaluating my dreams and goals. I'd begun to think that no one felt the emotions I experienced. Now I've discovered that chasing your dream is universal!*
> —Kentuckian

# Discovering Your Dream

There are two kinds of people in this world: dream pursuers and dream deniers. Which one are you?

Hold on a second! Did that question take you off guard? Do you find it difficult to assign yourself to one of those two categories? The plain truth is that everyone on earth has a dream. Everyone. Test it out for yourself: Ask friends and strangers what thing they would most love to do with their lives. You'll see eyes light up. You'll hear wistful sighs. And that person will display for you the most precious thing he or she nurtures inside.

But if we all have dreams, then why are so few of us actively pursuing them? "Because it's impossible," you say. Sure it is! That's what makes it a dream. The trouble is, we know in our hearts that nothing is impossible; that with God, there are no limits at all.

We can find a thousand reasons not to pursue our dreams. But could it just possibly be that there is one overwhelming reason we should go after it? Could it be that this beautiful, wonderful, and absolutely personal dream was planted there by Someone who knows you and loves you best? Could it be that we are all brothers and sisters, children of the Dream Giver whose one Magnificent Dream is made up of all the dreams and visions He has placed within us?

Imagine that! Your dream as one puzzle piece in a timeless, eternal, global and godly picture of a world beyond our dreams: the world of the Dream Giver.

And here's some good news: there is a road map—a beaten path—for the Dream Journey. Maybe you've been holding back because you felt as if you'd be launching into some foggy unknown. In this session you will learn the identifiable journey of the dream quest . . .

The Dream Journey will lead us through seven very different lands.

The first is all about *embracing the dream*. This is that space on the board game of life that reads, "GO!" Yet we linger there for years—perhaps a lifetime. In this particular session we'll learn how to identify the genuine dream within us, claim it as our destiny—and go!

The second portion is a very familiar place called your *Comfort Zone*. That's the place where you plant roots because you find life safe and predictable. Just beyond the borders of your zone, an adventure beckons to you. But first we come to a new place known as the *Borderland*. It is inhabited by people (often friends and family) who subtly try to bully us back into the comfort zone.

The fourth area is about finally going after our heart's desire—and finding it more difficult than we expected. As a matter of fact, this a lonely place we call the *Wasteland*. We're going to discover how to come through this wilderness into the power of a higher plain we call *Sanctuary*. Just as our hearts grow faint, we are invited to know the heart of the Dream Giver who will supply our every need.

The peace of Sanctuary is only broken by the threat of *Giants* in the land—the real-world challenges that threaten to derail the dream for which we have paid such a price. But now, stronger and wiser from our time with the Dream Giver, we are ready to stand and fight.

There remains only the *Land of Promise*: the fulfillment of our dream. But a surprise awaits us: this land becomes a new comfort zone! New dreams beckon; new adventures await; and as always, the Dream Giver smiles and leads us deeper into the secrets of His eternal kingdom.

Are you ready for the journey of a lifetime?

# QUOTES

*You see things; and you say, 'Why?'*
*But I dream things that never were;*
*and I say, "Why not?"*
—GEORGE BERNARD SHAW

*Through two years of searching and The Dream Giver,*
*piece by piece God laid out to me a dream called "Soul Saver*
*Ministries." Now a three part vision is coming to light.*
—A PEOPLE-LOVER

*Dreams come true; without that possibility,*
*nature would not incite us to have them.*
—JOHN UPDIKE

## Instructions

Before viewing the video, read "The Purpose" and "The Promise" in this workbook session. Then watch the video and take notes on anything you want to remember or want to discuss with others.

After watching the video, go to "My Own Journey" to evaluate where you are in your own Dream Journey. If you are meeting with a group, and time allows, go through the questions in "My Group's Journey" for further discussion.

During the week, review "The Principles", "The Pitfalls", and "The Pattern", to learn even more about each stage of the Dream Journey.


## Video Notes:

_____

_____

_____

_____

_____

_____

_____

_____

_____

_____

_____

_____

_____

_____

## The Purpose:

Discover the truth about your dreams, and the seven key stages of the Dream Journey.

## The Promise:

*The LORD had said to Abram, "Leave your country, your people and your father's household and go to the land I will show you. I will make you into a great nation and I will bless you; I will make your name great, and you will be a blessing. I will bless those who bless you, and whoever curses you I will curse; and all peoples on earth will be blessed through you."* GENESIS 12:1-3

*By faith Abraham, when called to go to a place he would later receive as his inheritance, obeyed and went, even though he did not know where he was going. By faith he made his home in the promised land like a stranger in a foreign country; he lived in tents ...* HEBREWS 11:8-9A

## The Principles

**1. We feel deep and profound emotions about our dreams.**

*"You have made known to me the path of life."* PSALM 16:11A

**2. The dream is built into us; it is the thing we were meant to do.**

*"Before I formed you in the womb I knew you, before you were born I set you apart."* JEREMIAH 1:5

**3. Dreams give us hope and purpose.**

*"Although I am less than the least of all God's people, this grace was given me: to preach to the Gentiles the unsearchable riches of Christ ..."* EPHESIANS 3:8

## The Pitfalls

Myths and misconceptions about discovering your dream.

**1. "A Dream isn't for people like me."**
*Truth: The Dream-Giver places dreams within each of us.*
*". . . everyone who is called by my name, whom I created for my glory, whom I formed and made."* ISAIAH 43:7

**2. "A Dream isn't possible for me."**
*Truth: Everyone has the opportunity to pursue his or her dream.*

*"What is impossible with men is possible with God."* LUKE 18:27B

## The Pattern

There are identifiable stages in pursuing your dream. In upcoming sessions, we will explore each of these lands and challenges faced by everyone who pursues a dream. There are no shortcuts on this map!

### 1. Discover the Dream.

*People who say such things show that they are . . . longing for a better country—a heavenly one. Therefore God is not ashamed to be called their God, for he has prepared a city for them.* HEBREWS 11:14A, 16

### 2. Move Out of the Comfort Zone.

*"Have I not commanded you? Be strong and courageous. Do not be terrified; do not be discouraged, for the LORD your God will be with you wherever you go."* JOSHUA 1:9

### 3. Escape the Bullies on the Borderland.

*And they spread among the Israelites a bad report about the land they had explored. They said, "The land we explored devours those living in it. All the people we saw there are of great size."* NUMBERS 13:32

### 4. Persevere through the Wasteland.

*"Consider it pure joy, my brothers, whenever you face trials of many kinds, because you know that the testing of your faith develops perseverance. Perseverance must finish its work so that you may be mature and complete, not lacking anything."* JAMES 1:2-4

### 5. Find Sanctuary at the Dream-Giver's invitation.

*"Delight yourself in the LORD and he will give you the desires of your heart. Commit your way to the LORD; trust in him and he will do this . . . Be still before the LORD and wait patiently for him."* PSALM 37:4-5, 7A

### 6. Stand tall against the Giants in the land.

*"For the eyes of the LORD range throughout the earth to strengthen those whose hearts are fully committed to him."* 2 CHRONICLES 16:9A

### 7. Enter the Land of Promise . . . and look to the horizon for the next dream!

*"So here I am today, eighty-five years old! . . . Now give me this hill country that the LORD promised me that day. You yourself heard then that the Anakites were there and their cities were large and fortified, but, the LORD helping me, I will drive them out just as he said."* JOSHUA 14:10C, 12

## My Own Journey

This is a page for personal evaluation and commitment. Think, pray, and reflect over each item before writing your answer. Then make a personal commitment to take action over the next few days.

1. My personal dream is:_____.

2. For me, the most compelling truth from this session was: _____

_____.

This was because: _____

_____.

3. What I have done to pursue my dream:_____

_____.

4. Obstacles (within me and outside) that have discouraged me from pursuing my dream:_____

_____.

5. Of the seven stages on the journey, I would locate myself: _____

_____.

6. I feel moved and inspired to take the following steps down the road of my Dream Journey:

How:_____

When:_____

Who to tell: _____


Signature_____ Date _____

*(Write your commitment in this box, then sign and date it.)*

## My Group's Journey

If you set aside a time for group discussion during this session, use these questions to help you consider the material.

1. Do you agree that every person has a dream? Why do you think this is so?

2. Read Genesis 12:1-4a. In this conversation between Abram and God, what elements of a dream can you identify?

3. Read Hebrews 11:8-9a. Again, what can we learn about dreams? What part does faith play in pursuing a dream?

4. In what ways would your life be different if you began to pursue your dream? What would be exciting for you? What would be challenging for you?

5. What is your greatest hope for this course? What commitments will you make to ensure that the course is as effective as possible for your group?

# This Is Your Dream

It seems as if it's always been there—your dream: a part of you, and yet independent of you. How could that be?

In one way, that dream is etched into your very being. It's as natural as your eye color or the talents you were born with. But in another way, that dream seems as if it came from outside. It's just there, in and of itself—not something you worked out on your own. You have made many important decisions about where to go and what to do in your life. But the dream stole in quietly, all by itself, and made a permanent home in your soul.

This thing called the dream is fascinating and unique, isn't it? Could it be that God, the Dream Giver, has something to do with that? Could it be that He has a dream for every living person, and He places it deep within us, even as He molds our personality around it? Yes! Another word for it might be purpose—but that doesn't have the same musical ring to it, does it? Dream is an emotional word for an emotional subject. It's the sum of our deepest, most optimistic, sky-high hopes.

It's an idea that simply pulses with power like an electric current: a vision of you doing something, even though you have never before done it. And when you think about it, there are also currents of joy and excitement. This is the life—the dreamscape that God has painted on the canvas of your soul.

Call it what you will—a purpose, a calling, a sacred destiny—but it's a thing that won't go away. Therefore, we might as well find out all that we can about it. And that includes understanding some of the myths and misconceptions about your dream.

The first of those is that a true and appropriate dream is sensible and logical. At least everyone tells us so, but you may already see the problem here: if the dream were so convenient, we would already have achieved it. No, the immediate problem with dreams is that they are too big! Well-meaning advisors also tell us that if that dream is for us, we will know exactly how to do it—or God will show us.

But we will grow elderly and frustrated if we wait for that simple formula to come on its own. This is where faith comes in; this is where personal growth comes in. Part of the dream adventure is the inner transformation God brings, and that includes living on the borderline of uncertainty at times. You must commit to the dream before all the how-tos are available to you.

We will also learn that dreams are based in human need—not so much ours, but the needs of a hurting world. God gives us His heart and emotions toward those in need. And we discover that fulfilling that passionate dream comes at great cost. We will be called upon to pay a price. But if this is our true dream, we will make those sacrifices—and we will enter a wonderful land of promise fulfillment.

> When a dream takes hold of you,
> what can you do? You can run with it, let it
> run your life, or let it go and think for the rest
> of your life about what might have been.
> —Patch Adams

# QUOTES

*Nobody succeeds beyond his or her wildest expectations
unless he or she begins with some wild expectations.*
—RALPH CHARELL

*My dream is a non-profit ministry called 'Healing Hearts
Foundation', honoring our elders. I want to help people
ages 66 and over achieve their own final dreams.
Keep dreaming everyone!*
— A WISH-GRANTER

*As a single parent, I always wanted to open a Day Care Center
to help other single parents finish school, go to college
or get a job to raise their children. I was recently injured,
and through that time God restored my body, soul,
and mind to prepare me to follow my dream.
The Dream Giver is leading the way!*
—GAIL

*I couldn't find the sports car of my dreams,
so I built it myself.*
—DR. FERDINAND PORSCHE

## Instructions

Before viewing the video, read "The Purpose" and "The Promise" in this workbook session. Then watch the video and take notes on anything you want to remember or want to discuss with others.

After watching the video, go to "My Own Journey" to evaluate where you are in your own Dream Journey. If you are meeting with a group, and time allows, go through the questions in "My Group's Journey" for further discussion.

During the week, review "The Principles", "The Pitfalls", and "The Pattern", to learn even more about each stage of the Dream Journey.

## Video Notes:

_____

_____

_____

_____

_____

_____

_____

_____

_____

_____

_____

_____

_____

## The Purpose:

Discover the nature of a personal dream, and how we can identify our own.

## The Promise:

*"The word of the LORD came to me, saying, 'Before I formed you in the womb I knew you, before you were born I set you apart; I appointed you as a prophet to the nations.'"* JEREMIAH 1:4-5

*For God does speak—now one way, now another— though man may not perceive it. In a dream, in a vision of the night, when deep sleep falls on men as they slumber in their beds, he may speak in their ears.* JOB 33:14-16A

## The Principles

1. **The dream begins in your heart in the "Land of Familiar"; it points you toward its fulfillment in the "Land of Promise."**

   *"Not that I have already obtained all this, or have already been made perfect, but I press on to take hold of that for which Christ Jesus took hold of me."* PHILIPPIANS 3:12

2. **The dream is a "sacred destiny," your personal calling.**

   *For we are God's workmanship, created in Christ Jesus to do good works, which God prepared in advance for us to do.* EPHESIANS 2:10

3. **The dream is one part of the Dream-Giver's great dream for all of us.**

   *And we know that in all things God works for the good of those who love him, who have been called according to his purpose.* ROMANS 8:28

---

> *What we need is more people who specialize in the impossible.*
> —Theodore Roethke

## The Pitfalls

Myths and misconceptions about the dream.

### 1. "The dream is only for an extraordinary person."

*Truth: Every human being is a dreamer.*

*". . . Everyone who is called by my name, whom I created for my glory, whom I formed and made."* ISAIAH 43:7

### 2. "The dream should *be* sensible and realistic."

*Truth: Genuine dreams are always over-sized and daunting.*

*"I will make you into a great nation . . . and all peoples on earth will be blessed through you."* GENESIS 12:2A, 3B

### 3. "The dream requires our readiness before our commitment."

*Truth: If we wait until we know how to fulfill it, we will never start.*

*"Now faith is being sure of what we hope for and certain of what we do not see. This is what the ancients were commended for."* HEBREWS 11:1-2

## The Pattern

Four Stages in Discovering Your Dream

### 1. Selfish: *The dream meets my needs.*

### 2. Shared: *The dream meets our needs.*

### 3. Sacrificial: *The dream meets your needs.*

### 4. Sacred: *The dream serves God.*

How can I identify my dream?

- Pay attention to need wherever you find it.

- Pay attention to your talents.

- Pay attention to your passions and desires.

- Pay attention to your spirit (your relationship with God).

You are the steward of your dream. It is placed in your trust. What does the Dream Giver want you to do about it?

*"Teach us to number our days aright, that we may gain a heart of wisdom."*
PSALM 90:12

# My Own Journey

This is your personal page. After you have completed this session of *The Dream Giver* curriculum, work through these questions in order to make your personal commitment to put your dreams into action.

1. From this session, my most important new insight into my own dream was: _____

_____.

2. My key misconception (pitfall) in relation to the dream has been:

_____

_____.

3. As I look at the four stages of dream development (selfish, shared, sacrificial, sacred), I feel I am at the _____ stage. Here is why:

_____

_____.

4. I expect to move to the next stage by:_____.

5. As I reflect carefully upon the four keys to identifying my dream, the strongest point I discover about myself is: _____

_____.

---

6. I feel that the Dream Giver is leading me to take the following action as soon as possible:

What: _____

When:_____

Who to tell: _____

Signature_____ Date _____

*(Write your commitment in this box, then sign and date it.)*

## My Group's Journey

If you set aside a time for group discussion during this session, use these questions to help you consider the material.

1. Some of us can quickly describe our dream; others are uncertain. In your opinion, what are the greatest challenges in attempting to identify one's dream?

2. Read Jeremiah 1:4-5. What do you feel is significant about God's timetable in assigning tasks and missions to His children?

3. When you reflect on God planning for you before you before you were born, how do you feel about His emotions toward you? How does it affect your dream?

4. What is the most important insight found in Job 33:14-16a? What are some of the various ways ("now one way, now another") that God impresses upon us our dreams? How has He done so in your life?

5. Hebrews 11:1-2 offers an intriguing definition of faith. Put the meaning in your own words. What does it say to you about the fulfillment of your dream?

# Your Comfort Zone

You may not remember the very first time you entered a pool of water. Perhaps your mother or father held you tight, you wrapped your arms around that parent's neck, and the two of you stepped into the cool, mysterious fluid.

But if you later learned to swim, that memory is probably a vivid one for you. What a trial! You could dip your toes into a few inches of water, but the deeper areas were as terrifying as the edge of the world. You were uncomfortable even being near the deeper water.

Then perhaps some patient, wise, and older person showed you how to tread water. There was a terrible moment when you let your feet leave the security of the firm earth beneath, and you wondered if your head would really stay above the surface.

And still there was so much more to learn! How did you ever do it? Learning to swim forced you out of one comfort zone after another, farther and farther from the safe haven of dry land. People were not designed to live like fish; why would anyone go to such trouble to learn to propel himself or herself through the depths?

The answer is simple: the adventure is well worthwhile, as any swimmer knows. There is no feeling quite like plunging into cool water on a hot day. But like the rest of the life, that adventure comes at a price: we must venture to the edge of the Land of Familiar, walk right up to the border of uncertainty, and take that suspenseful step.

Here is the very reason we see so few dream chasers in this world of dreamers. The vast majority of humanity cannot bring itself to step outside its comfort zone. But think about it: what is life but one great, expanding frontier of comfort zones? Everything you've ever earned, everything that ever meant something to you, involved some level of venturing into the Land of Unfamiliar: learning to walk; the first day of school; the first romantic date; the new job; marriage.

At times we look back and realize we have ventured to places in life we never expected. But various pressures pushed us into those steps. The real adventure—the one we nurture in our hearts, and the one that brings a tingle down the spine when we think of it—that one remains out of reach, because the usual social pressures are not there.

A shepherd boy named David once stated, rather matter-of-factly, that he had killed a bear and a lion; why retreat from a giant? (1 Samuel 17:37) Why indeed? If you have conquered X and Y, why stop short of Z, when you know in your heart that Z is your Big One—the one you were placed in this world to attain.

David's reasoning was simple: It was God who gave the victories over the beasts in his path. Is any challenge too great for God? That boy had the right idea: the Dream Giver not only wants you to be bold and move out, but He promises to go with you.

In this session, let's discover how to escape the Comfort Zone.

*People are never more insecure
than when they become obsessed with
their fears at the expense of their dreams.*
—Norman Cousins

# QUOTES

*I'm like Ordinary—reluctant to leave Familiar. Being a single parent with two children makes me fear leaving Familiar to pursue my dreams. But the Dream Giver is leading me on.*

—ANGIE

*Fear is a darkroom where negatives develop.*

—USMAN ASIF

*After the death of a parent, the loss of a child, and a constant fear of rejection and disapproval, I asked God to do whatever needs to be done within me, so His spiritual vision for my life can become a natural reality.*

—NEW YORKER

## Instructions

Before viewing the video, read "The Purpose" and "The Promise" in this workbook session. Then watch the video and take notes on anything you want to remember or want to discuss with others.

After watching the video, go to "My Own Journey" to evaluate where you are in your own Dream Journey. If you are meeting with a group, and time allows, go through the questions in "My Group's Journey" for further discussion.

During the week, review "The Principles", "The Pitfalls", and "The Pattern", to learn even more about each stage of the Dream Journey.

## Video Notes:

_____

_____

_____

_____

_____

_____

_____

_____

_____

_____

_____

_____

_____

_____

## The Purpose:

Discover the traits of your own Comfort Zone, and learn how to move past its borders.

## The Promise:

*But Moses said to God, "Who am I, that I should go to Pharaoh and bring the Israelites out of Egypt?" And God said, "I will be with you."* EXODUS 3:11-12A

*[Moses said:] "Be strong and courageous. Do not be afraid or terrified because of them, for the LORD your God goes with you; he will never leave you nor forsake you . . . The LORD himself goes before you and will be with you; he will never leave you nor forsake you. Do not be afraid; do not be discouraged."* DEUTERONOMY 31:6, 8

## The Principles

1. **The Comfort Zone lies between you and the attainment of your dream.** Following your dream involves discomfort.

2. **The Comfort Zone is a defense mechanism when we face change.** It comes from inside us, and its key symptom is fear.

## The Pitfalls

Myths and misconceptions about the Comfort Zone.

1. **"My Comfort Zone fear is unique to me."**
   *Truth: it is universal.*
   *"Therefore, since we are surrounded by such a great cloud of witnesses, let us throw off everything that hinders and the sin that so easily entangles, and let us run with perseverance the race marked out for us."* HEBREWS 12:1

2. **"My Comfort Zone fear means the dream must be unacceptable."**
   *Truth: It is natural and human—a sign you are on the right path.*
   *"[Jesus] took Peter and the two sons of Zebedee along with him, and he began to be sorrowful and troubled. Then he said to them, 'My soul is overwhelmed with sorrow to the point of death. Stay here and keep watch with me.' Going a little farther, he fell with his face to the ground and prayed, 'My Father, if it is possible, may this cup be taken from me. Yet not as I will, but as you will.'"*
   MATTHEW 26:37-39

# The Pattern

**1. Comfort Zones are justified because we feel unworthy.**

*"But Moses said to God, 'Who am I, that I should go to Pharaoh?'"*
EXODUS 3:11

**2. Comfort Zones are rationalized because we feel unable.**

*"Moses said to the LORD, 'O Lord, I have never been eloquent, neither in the past nor since you have spoken to your servant. I am slow of speech and tongue'."* EXODUS 4:10

**3. Comfort Zones are solidified because we choose to be unwilling.**

*"But Moses said, 'O Lord, please send someone else to do it'."* EXODUS 4:13

**4. Comfort Zones are overcome when you adopt victorious attitudes:**

*a. Value the dream more than your comfort.*

*"If they had been thinking of the country they had left, they would have had opportunity to return. Instead, they were longing for a better country—a heavenly one."* HEBREWS 11:15-16A

*b. Accept the inevitable possibility of failing.*

*"Endure hardship as discipline; God is treating you as sons."* HEBREWS 12:7A

*c. Choose to be strong and courageous, and make a decision not to turn back—a commitment with no escape clause—that you will never again imprison yourself in the Comfort Zone.*

*"The LORD himself goes before you and will be with you; he will never leave you nor forsake you. Do not be afraid; do not be discouraged."* DEUTERONOMY 31:8

*Courage is fear that has said its prayers.*
—Dorothy Bernard

# My Own Journey

This is your personal page. After you have completed the Comfort Zone session, work through these questions in order to make your personal commitment to put your own fears behind you.

1. When I hear about the Comfort Zone, the first thing I think of from my own life is: _____.

2. On a scale of 1-10 (10 being the boldest), I would rate my "discomfort threshold" (willingness to live and move forward while uncomfortable) as: _____.

Here are my comments about why: _____

_____.

3. Moses felt unworthy, unable, and unwilling. The one I identify most with is _____.

Here is why: _____.

4. On a scale of 1-10 (10 being the most eager and excited) here is how I rate my willingness to move forward immediately and put my Comfort Zone behind me: _____.

Comments: _____.

5. If I were to talk with God about the emotions I feel right now, I think He would say: _____.

6. I feel that the Dream Giver is leading me to take the following action as soon as possible:

What: _____

When: _____

Who to tell: _____

Signature _____ Date _____

*(Write your commitment in this box, then sign and date it.)*

## My Group's Journey

If you set aside a time for group discussion during this session, use these questions to help you consider the material.

1. As a group, compare and contrast each member's key Comfort Zone issue (to the extent that each member feels comfortable sharing).

2. Read Exodus 3:11; 4:10; 4:13. Which of these responses do you believe is the most common to people facing uncertainty? Why?

3. How does God respond to each of these emotions and assumptions?

4. Discuss as a group the true risks you would face by going beyond your Comfort Zone. How would you evaluate these compared to the possible reward?

5. Divide into groups of two, and spend your remaining time sharing individual commitments to break free of the Comfort Zone. Pray for each other, asking God to make each person strong and of good courage.

# The Borderland

**P**ursuing your dream may be many things, but predictable is not one of them.

The Dream Giver seems to have a new surprise at every turn. It is surprising to learn that your true dream is not just an idle fantasy, but a sacred destiny from the loving hand of God. It is surprising to learn that the first obstacle is that person in the mirror. The greatest dream-killer is the fear inside us.

And then, when we finally make it by those inner dragons, another surprise awaits us. We find that the new barrier is other people—people we thought were on our side.

Imagine the scene. At get-together for your closest friends and family, you call for everyone's attention. You announce your new priority in life: following your dream. Instead of applause, there is an awkward silence. Your spouse angrily leaves the room. Your mother begins telling you she would hate to see you set yourself up for disappointment. Your best friend is enumerating reasons you should not even think about this new quest.

If the dream is the light of your inner life, why can't these people see that? Why don't they want you to pursue the one course you've longed to follow? Why can't they see what you see—the world as it will look when your goals have been reached?

You have come to a very tense place we call the Borderland. Borderlands are places where countries intersect, and history is filled with battles over them.

The fact is that your dream pushes out the borders until they overlap someone else's territory. For example, your dream may be to accomplish something exciting—begin a new and ambitious business—but your parents have a dream for you, too, and it's not the same vision: they merely want you to be safe, secure, and stable. You can handle the risk of failure, but they cannot. This is because they love you, of course, but someone's dream for your life has to recede: theirs or yours.

And so we feel intimidated. We feel nudged and shoved backward, back to the Land of Familiar, back to the Comfort Zone. And we might begin to feel that God, the Dream Giver, is speaking through these people to tell us that we have chosen the wrong dream. This conclusion would be a terrible mistake, for the truth is that every great pursuit encounters resistance at the Borderland. You might say it "comes with the territory."

It's one more obstacle in the quest for our dream, but the good news is this: every barrier makes us stronger, makes us wiser, teaches us more about ourselves and brings us a little bit closer to that great goal that lies before us. Not every loved one will endorse your dream, but in time, some of them will begin to share your dream. Some will open doors for you. And when those around you reveal their own dreams, you'll know exactly what the Dream Giver wants you to say and do for your friend.

You can be a Dream Enabler for many people around you. And that's one more dream come true.

> *I* now realize that even Christian friends can be Border Bullies! If I'm not meant to live this dream, why do I often cry when I dream about it? I'm resolving to walk in faith, be courageous and trust God to get me over the border.
> —Sharon

# QUOTES

*If at first you don't succeed,*
*you'll get a lot of free advice*
*from folks who didn't succeed either.*

—ANONYMOUS

*I don't know the recipe for success,*
*but the recipe for failure*
*is to try and please everybody.*

—BILL COSBY

*Hey, these are people I love! I know they feel they're protecting me*
*from uncertainty. I do want to please them, but this dream just*
*won't let go! I never thought my family and friends*
*could be obstacles.*

—BORDERLINE DREAMER

*The world is moving so fast these days*
*that the man who says it can't be done*
*is generally interrupted by someone doing it.*

—HARRY EMERSON FOSDICK

## Instructions

Before viewing the video, read "The Purpose" and "The Promise" in this workbook session. Then watch the video and take notes on anything you want to remember or want to discuss with others.

After watching the video, go to "My Own Journey" to evaluate where you are in your own Dream Journey. If you are meeting with a group, and time allows, go through the questions in "My Group's Journey" for further discussion.

During the week, review "The Principles", "The Pitfalls", and "The Pattern", to learn even more about each stage of the Dream Journey.

## Video Notes:

_____

_____

_____

_____

_____

_____

_____

_____

_____

_____

_____

_____

_____

_____

_____

## The Purpose:

Discover the truth about intimidators who try to block our dream pursuit.

## The Promise:

*"And they spread among the Israelites a bad report about the land they had explored. They said, 'The land we explored devours those living in it. All the people we saw there are of great size . . . We seemed like grasshoppers in our own eyes, and we looked the same to them'."* NUMBERS 13:32, 33B

*"Fear of man will prove to be a snare, but whoever trusts in the LORD is kept safe."* PROVERBS 29:25

## The Principles

1. **Borderland is the space where Comfort Zones overlap.**

2. **Borderland attracts people whom your dream affects.**

3. **Borderland is the boundary of other people's "walls of fear".**

If the Comfort Zone is our prison, those in the Borderland are the "prison guards" or Border Patrol.

- Border Bullies are those who attempt to push us back toward our Comfort Zones.

  *"Coming to his hometown, [Jesus] began teaching the people in their synagogue, and they were amazed. 'Where did this man get this wisdom and these miraculous powers?' they asked. 'Isn't this the carpenter's son?' And they took offense at him. But Jesus said to them, 'Only in his hometown and in his own house is a prophet without honor.'"* MATTHEW 13:54-55A, 57

- Border Buddies are those who neither encourage or discourage us.

- Border Busters are those who open doors for us, speeding us onward toward the dream.

  *[Paul the Apostle writes:] "James, Peter and John, those reputed to be pillars, gave me and Barnabas the right hand of fellowship when they recognized the grace given to me. They agreed that we should go to the Gentiles, and they to the Jews."* GALATIANS 2:9

## The Pitfalls

Myths and misconceptions about the Borderland.

1. **"Those around me will share my dream."**
   *Truth: Others' Comfort Zones will intersect with yours, and these people will be threatened in some way by your dream.*

2. **"I won't be bruised by conflicts on the Borderland."**
   *Truth: These conflicts can last for years, and be very damaging to our hearts and our aspirations.*

## The Pattern

1. **Border Bullies exaggerate the dangers.**
   *And they spread among the Israelites a bad report about the land they had explored. They said, 'The land we explored devours those living in it. All the people we saw there are of great size'.* NUMBERS 13:32

2. **Border Bullies complain about the difficulties.**
   *They gave Moses this account: 'We went into the land to which you sent us . . . But the people who live there are powerful, and the cities are fortified and very large.'* NUMBERS 13:27A, 28A

3. **Border Bullies idealize the "good old days."**
   *And again the Israelites started wailing and said, 'If only we had meat to eat! . . . But now we have lost our appetite; we never see anything but this manna!'* NUMBERS 11:4B, 6

4. **Become a Border Buster for Others**
   *"Do not let any unwholesome talk come out of your mouths, but only what is helpful for building others up according to their needs, that it may benefit those who listen."* EPHESIANS 4:29

## My Own Journey

This is your personal page. After you have completed the Borderland session, work through these questions in order to make your personal commitment to break through the border to your dream.

1. The following describes my current or most memorable experience with "border bullies": _____

_____.

Here is the way that person's Comfort Zone overlapped mine: _____

_____.

2. Based upon the 4 patterns of border bully behavior on page 36, the one I have encountered most is: _____.

3. Here is a complete list of the people who are—or may become—border bullies as I pursue my dream: _____

_____.

Here are some "border busters" who may help me pursue my dream:

_____.

4. I believe the best way for me to deal lovingly with the border bullies in my life, while still moving forward with my dream, would be: ____

_____.

5. I realize there are others around me who are processing their own dreams. I would most closely identify myself as a __ border bully; __ border buddy; __ border buster. Here is the name of one person whom I can help to pursue his or her dream: _____.

---

6. I hereby commit myself not to be intimidated by border bullies, but to lovingly defend my dream and move toward reaching it.

Signature_____ Date _____

*(Write your commitment in this box, then sign and date it.)*

---

## My Group's Journey

If you set aside a time for group discussion during this session, use these questions to help you consider the material.

1. The video presentation offers a skit that demonstrates various kinds of people who discourage us from our dreams. Allow each person in the group to share a) which one they recognized most; and b) which one they are the most like in relation to others' dreams.

2. Read Numbers 13:32-33. To what extent were the ten spies being realistic? What were they lacking in their perspective?

3. Read Proverbs 29:25. A snare is a hidden trap for unwary creatures. How does fear become a snare for border bullies? For dreamers intimidated by the bullies?

4. Galatians 2:9 shows how fellow believers encouraged Paul's dream of bringing the gospel to the Gentiles. What are some guidelines for "recognizing the grace" in our friends' dreams, so that we can be border busters?

5. In groups of two or three, spend your remaining time formulating plans for handling difficult relationships with those on the borders of our dream pursuits.

# The Wasteland

Abraham, trusting and obedient, dreamed of a child. So he waited . . . and waited . . . as the decades rolled past. The Israelites dreamed of a land of milk and honey within a few days' walk—but it took 40 years to get there.

David dreamed of a palace, but waited for years in a cave. Joseph dreamed of becoming one of the world's great men, but years of slavery and prison came first. Even Jesus spent time in the wilderness; hungry, thirsty, and tested to the limits of endurance—in a wasteland that bordered his ministry field of dreams.

Each entered his own Promised Land, but only at the far side of a dark valley. So why are we always so surprised when we find ourselves in our own private wilderness?

The first great and terrible truth about the Wasteland is that when it appears, it swallows your horizon. You cannot go around it, over it, or under it—you must trudge right through it.

But we arrive there when we least expect it, just after we have overcome the inertia within us and the discouragers around us. For one brief moment, it seems as if blue skies and green pastures lay ahead. We can almost reach out and touch the shining star we have dreamed of.

It's too early to celebrate. This is just the moment when things grind to a halt. Suddenly we are up facing a wall that will not move. We use all our energy in devising schemes to break through, leap over, dig under, or make an end run. But nothing works. The dream is delayed.

During the painful days that follow, the only progress we make is from disappointment to devastation. In the heat of the desert, the dream begins to feel as if was just another mirage. Maybe our friends were right. Maybe God sent the wrong person.

Our thoughts turn nostalgically to the Land of Familiar. Why not give it up, retire, and fluff up our pillows in a nice Comfort Zone?

Yet giving up would mean something fragile and beautiful would die inside us. Shattered dream, shattered spirit. Surrender now and we'll pass our lives in quiet desperation.

No, we're wiser than that. Wiser, stronger, and more patient. We believe the dream is no mirage. It's more real than any temporary hardship. The real mirage is the idea of waste in Wasteland. This has been no waste! It's been all about testing, growing, toughening up. This has been the harsh flame that tempers the iron. And the iron will make fine armor when we face down those giants, within a prayer of the Promise.

On the rock of that hope we persevere. For now, the Wasteland must be faced and the dream must be delayed. Is it fun? Certainly not! Endurable? Yes, by the grace of God. We endure it as we endure the trials and testing that life brings us, on the rocky road to becoming the powerful, victorious and righteous warriors God intends. And at the end, we will stand tall in the Hall of Champions—with Moses, David, and all the others—and realize that this season of tears made the triumph all the sweeter.

> *The Promised Land always lies*
> *on the other side of a Wilderness.*
> —Havelock Ellis

# QUOTES

*Quite often the absence of immediate success
is the mark of a genuine call.*

—BRUCE LARSON

*When written in Chinese, the word 'crisis' is composed
of 2 characters. One represents danger,
and the other represents opportunity.*

—JOHN F. KENNEDY

*My dream is to work with pre-teens and young adults with
behavior disorders. I can see now that God is teaching me even
in the dust storm. Today's lesson is patience!*

—A "WHIRLWIND" RIDER

*There are some days, in the middle of the wasteland, when it
feels like there is never going to be a Land of Promise. I'm on
chemotherapy, but my oncologist has given the okay for me to go
on a missions trip this summer to Thailand and Singapore.
I want to be used by God—no matter what.*

—JESSICA

## Instructions

Before viewing the video, read "The Purpose" and "The Promise" in this workbook session. Then watch the video and take notes on anything you want to remember or want to discuss with others.

After watching the video, go to "My Own Journey" to evaluate where you are in your own Dream Journey. If you are meeting with a group, and time allows, go through the questions in "My Group's Journey" for further discussion.

During the week, review "The Principles", "The Pitfalls", and "The Pattern", to learn even more about each stage of the Dream Journey.

## Video Notes:

_____

_____

_____

_____

_____

_____

_____

_____

_____

_____

_____

_____

_____

_____

## The Purpose

To discover the truth about the discouraging stage of dream pursuit known as the Wasteland, and to learn how to persevere through it.

## The Promise

*Consider it pure joy, my brothers, whenever you face trials of many kinds, because you know that the testing of your faith develops perseverance. Perseverance must finish its work so that you may be mature and complete, not lacking anything.* JAMES 1:2-4

*And we know that in all things God works for the good of those who love him, who have been called according to his purpose . . . What, then, shall we say in response to this? If God is for us, who can be against us?* ROMANS 8:28, 31

## The Principles

1. **The Wasteland Wedge:** We are frustrated by our awareness of the growing gap between expectations and reality. By our own timetable, we should be much farther along.

2. **The Wasteland focuses on the dreamer's preparation.**
   - Capacity is enlarged.
   - Character is strengthened.
   - Confidence is developed.
   - Consistency is built.
   - Competence is improved.
   - Calling is clarified.
   - Communion with God is deepened.

   *Examples: David and Joseph.*

   *Truths from James 1:2-4:*
   - The Wasteland is necessary because we aren't ready.
   - The Wasteland calls us to be patient.

## 3. The Wasteland is proportionate to the size of the dream.

- Small dream, small Wasteland; larger dream, larger Wasteland.
- Wasteland is long, difficult, and multiple. God is maturing many different capacities and characteristics within us during this period.

# The Pitfalls

Myths and misconceptions about the Wasteland

### 1. "The Wasteland season is preventable."

*Truth: There is no way around it. It is an inevitable stage for the achievement of every dream.*

### 2. "The Wasteland season is purposeless."

*Truth: While it feels like a waste of time and energy, it a necessary stage of seasoning and preparation.*

# The Pattern

Emotional Stages of the Wasteland Wedge—depending on our response.

**1. Disappointment.** "I expected to make more progress."

**2. Determination.** "Maybe if I work harder?"

**3. Discouragement.** "Why can't I break out of this slump?"

**4. Doubt.** "Was I wrong about the dream?"

**5. Disillusionment.** "I didn't know the world was this way."

**6. Distress.*** "I am a failure."

**7. Double-mindedness.** "Maybe I'll continue, maybe not."

**8. Despair.** "I have no hope."

**9. Death of the dream.** "I give up."

*\*In the midst of the emotional turmoil of distress, we are highly susceptible to moral temptation and failure.*

## My Own Journey

This is your personal page. After you have completed the Wasteland session, work through these questions in order to make your personal commitment to persevere through the dry and difficult seasons of your dream pursuit.

1. When I think about my own personal strength in facing the Wasteland ahead, I would evaluate myself this way:_____

_____.

2. As I reflect upon my particular dream, I can imagine that my Wasteland would be something like this: _____

_____.

3. I realize that the Wasteland help me toward being "mature and complete, not lacking anything"(James 1:4). Here are the areas I would expect God to work the most:

❏ Capacity is enlarged.          ❏ Competence is improved.

❏ Character is strengthened.     ❏ Calling is clarified.

❏ Confidence is developed.       ❏ Communion with God

❏ Consistency is built.          is deepened.

4. Here are some ways I will gain strength from God to make it through the Wasteland: _____

_____.

5. Wasteland Covenant: "I believe the Wasteland is a necessary stage in my journey to fulfill the dream. I therefore place all my trust in the Dream Giver. I pledge to cooperate with Him fully in all the ways He works within and around me to prepare me for completion of the dream."

Signature_____ Date _____

*(When you have prayed and reflected upon this commitment, and fully agree with it, sign, date, and save it.)*

# My Group's Journey

If you set aside a time for group discussion during this session, use these questions to help you consider the material.

1. Which group members have encountered this Wasteland stage? Which are in it now? Discuss as a group.

2. Read James 1:2-4. What truths do you find encouraging about this passage? Which truths do you find most challenging? Why?

3. Do you think it is possible to find joy in discouragement, as this passage commands? How? Explain.

4. Read Romans 8:28, 31. What do we learn about God's process for our lives? How should we therefore look upon various advances and setbacks?

5. What can we do to help others through their trials and testing? Who needs help right now?

# Sanctuary

With grim determination you trudge onward toward your dream. It's amazing how strong is that spark of insistence within you. Just when you think you'll surely collapse, somehow you put one foot in front of the other once more, then again . . . and with head down, you resolutely soldier on through the Valley of the Shadow.

Then something odd occurs; a feeling that seems to have come from nowhere—a distinct impression that something has changed within you. You are not the same person who set out on this journey. You are wearier but stronger; sadder but wiser. Most of all, you are more sensitive, more perceptive of the quiet inner truths; things of the spirit.

Your inner reckoning seems sharper, and right now faintly perceives, though the desert dust, a green mountain to the side of your road. Your mind says to keep moving ahead, undistracted, onward to the battlefield for the final contest. But your heart discloses that something powerful and essential awaits you within the haze of that mountain. Yes, this is an important invitation, and even the dream must wait. Without clearly knowing why, you will climb this mountain that will become Sanctuary for you; a safe haven; a respite.

The truth is that, as you follow your dream, you will endure hardship of body, mind, and spirit. There will come a time for healing, clarification, and preparation for the last lap of the journey. This is a mountain on the by-way, a stage that could be ignored—but what a sad mistake that would be. You need rest; you need Sanctuary.

So you approach this lovely, misty mountain. This experience, you sense, will be unlike anything else in your pursuit of the dream or of life in general. As it unfolds, there will be three separate developments.

First, there will be a period of restoration, refreshment, and rejuvenation. It's like an icy waterfall tumbling from the mountain, creating a cool, clear pool. Your tears mingle with the living water that flows all over you, and the healing begins. Slowly you feel yourself becoming whole again, and the scars are beginning to disappear. Yes, you're glad you came.

But there is more. Your eyes move upward to a thick wall of ancient trees, where a blinding light pierces the gaps. You feel the irresistible tug at your heart as you are invited to climb onward and upward to investigate. Somehow you know that at the center of that light you will find the Dream Giver himself, and that he will perform the deepest healing yet.

But there is one final climb. As you reach the summit of that mountain, it seems as if you can see forever: the treacherous miles you have come, the Valley of the Giants ahead, the dream beyond. But you feel a hand on your shoulder, and you hear the voice of the Dream Giver saying, "Give me your dream." And you realize that this may well be the greatest of all the missions with which you have been charged.

Will you finally hand over your cherished dream to the one who made it? Welcome to Sanctuary, the deepest, most mysterious, most wonderful, adventure of the dream—and of life itself.

> *What makes the desert beautiful is that somewhere it hides a well.*
> —Antoine de Saint-Exupéry

# QUOTES

We never know when our disappointment
will be His appointment.
— CHARLES SWINDOLL

God whispers to us in our pleasures,
speaks in our conscience, but shouts in our pains.
—C. S. LEWIS

I am in sanctuary right now. Never before have I felt such great
peace and closeness to Our Lord. I desire with all my heart for
my dream to move forward, but for now I'm peaceful and content
being saturated with the Love of God. The next step is going to be
the most challenging of all, but I'm ready.
—LAURA

I've come to realize an amazing truth: I don't have to struggle so
much anymore. I can now step into my dream and walk in full
confidence that God's plan is going to happen. I can believe in
faith that He's leading me, regardless of my imperfections.
—JOSH

## Instructions

Before viewing the video, read "The Purpose" and "The Promise" in this workbook session. Then watch the video and take notes on anything you want to remember or want to discuss with others.

After watching the video, go to "My Own Journey" to evaluate where you are in your own Dream Journey. If you are meeting with a group, and time allows, go through the questions in "My Group's Journey" for further discussion.

During the week, review "The Principles", "The Pitfalls", and "The Pattern", to learn even more about each stage of the Dream Journey.

## Video Notes:

_____

_____

_____

_____

_____

_____

_____

_____

_____

_____

_____

_____

_____

# The Purpose

To discover the nature of a dreamer's opportunity to know the Dream Giver more deeply after the most difficult trials, and to learn about the three stages of that encounter.

# The Promise

*"Come to me, all you who are weary and burdened, and I will give you rest. Take my yoke upon you and learn from me, for I am gentle and humble in heart, and you will find rest for your souls. For my yoke is easy and my burden is light."*
MATTHEW 11:28-30

*Delight yourself in the LORD and he will give you the desires of your heart. Commit your way to the LORD; trust in him and he will do this . . . Be still before the LORD and wait patiently for him.*   PSALM 37:4-5, 7A

# The Pitfalls

Myths and Misconceptions about Sanctuary

## 1. "Requirement: I don't need to take time for Sanctuary."

*Truth: Those who hurry by, neglecting this healing retreat, will still be wounded and weary when they go into battle with the giant trials ahead.*

## 2. "Risk: I don't like being vulnerable—the feeling of being out of control."

*Truth: Sanctuary is in the hands of the Dream Giver, and the dreamer must risk the humbling experience of drawing near.*

# The Pattern and the Principles

The dreamer's decision to seek Sanctuary will lead to three more successive options, each more intensely transformational than the last.

## 1. Waterfall: Restoration.

As with a healing pool, our many Wasteland wounds are made whole again, one by one.

*"Come to me, all you who are weary and burdened, and I will give you rest. Take my yoke upon you and learn from me, for I am gentle and humble in heart, and you will find rest for your souls. For my yoke is easy and my burden is light."* MATTHEW 11:28-30

- Physical restoration.
- Emotional restoration.
- Spiritual restoration.

PURSUE THE RADICAL TRANSFORMATION OF SANCTUARY.

## 2. Light: Relationship.

The Dream Giver's radiance breaks through like the sun through trees, drawing us closer to him.

*"Delight yourself in the LORD and he will give you the desires of your heart. Commit your way to the LORD; trust in him and he will do this . . . Be still before the LORD and wait patiently for him."* PSALM 37:4-5, 7A

- Cleansing.
- Communion.
- Consistency.

## 3. Summit: Relinquishment.

The Dream Giver gently asks us to surrender the dream to his care, in order that the dream doesn't become more important than the Dream Giver.

*"I tell you the truth, unless a kernel of wheat falls to the ground and dies, it remains only a single seed. But if it dies, it produces many seeds. The man who loves his life will lose it, while the man who hates his life in this world will keep it for eternal life. Whoever serves me must follow me; and where I am, my servant also will be. My Father will honor the one who serves me."* JOHN 12:24-26

- You are the steward of the dream, not the owner.
- You are the servant of the Dream Giver, not the dream.

## 4. Pursue the radical transformation of Sanctuary.

*"The LORD is my shepherd, I shall not be in want. He makes me lie down in green pastures, he leads me beside quiet waters, he restores my soul. He guides me in paths of righteousness for his name's sake. Even though I walk through the valley of the shadow of death, I will fear no evil, for you are with me; your rod and your staff, they comfort me. You prepare a table before me in the presence of my enemies. You anoint my head with oil; my cup overflows. Surely goodness and love will follow me all the days of my life, and I will dwell in the house of the LORD forever."* PSALM 23

## My Own Journey

This is your personal page. After you have completed this session of The Dream Giver curriculum, work through these questions in order to make your personal commitment to put your dreams into action.

1. The insight about Sanctuary that I found most the most exciting was:

_____.

2. One time in my life when I experienced some of the aspects of Sanctuary was:_____

_____.

3. At this moment, the part of me (emotional, physical, or spiritual) that most needs healing is the following, and I will explain why:_____

_____.

4. One issue of my life or personality that would make it more difficult for me to draw near to the Dream Giver in Sanctuary is:_____

_____.

5. On  scale of 1-10, with 10 being the most humble and sacrificial, I would grade my own willingness to hand my dream over to the Dream Giver as \_\_\_\_ . Here is how I can raise my grade: _____

_____.

---

6. Having studied this session, reflected carefully and spent time with the Dream Giver, I feel that he is asking me to take the following action:.

What: _____

When:_____

Who to tell: _____

Signature_____ Date _____

*(Write your commitment in this box, then sign and date it.)*

## My Group's Journey

If you set aside a time for group discussion during this session, use these questions to help you consider the material.

1. In what ways is the Sanctuary stage significant in its placement—that is, as it follows Wasteland, and precedes facing the Giants who oppose our dreams?

2. Compare Matthew 11:28-30 with Luke 14:26-27, 33. Is it "easy" or "hard" to serve the Master? Explain your answer. Hint: Consider the "occasion" that is implied by each of these passages.

3. Read Psalm 37:4-5, 7a. Restate this exciting promise in your own words. Why should dreamers be particularly thrilled by these words? What part of the promise are we expected to keep?

4. As a group, review each of the three stages of Sanctuary. Then divide into groups of two and discuss occasions when each of you have experienced these truths.

5. Remaining in groups of two, close your session in prayer, each person offering a commitment to permanently and completely trust his or her dream to the Dream Giver.

# Valley Of The Giants

Half a century ago, a scientific debate raged over whether the speed of sound could be exceeded by a jet plane. Aero-designers bent over their drawing boards, dreaming up new vessels and fresh approaches that would "push the envelope," as they described it—surpass the known barriers for flight pressure. Tragically, many pilots died before the historic day in 1947 when test pilot Chuck Yeager survived a flight at over 662 miles per hour.

Such a flight is routine today. But a deadly struggle was the price for this ability. Men actually gave their lives. A generation earlier, it was the same story for those seeking to make the first trans-Atlantic air flight. The greater the goal, the more painful will be the sacrifice, and it must be paid out upon a final battlefield—the threshold of a dream's culmination.

Here may be the nightmare that comes with the dream. And the price seems too high. Even before that ultimate conflict, we feel we have offered considerable sacrifice. For a tall dream, we have given blood, sweat, and tears just to get this far. Haven't we already earned our rightful prize?

There is another reason we may be taken off guard. If we arrive fresh from the mountaintop experience of Sanctuary, we may be relaxed. We may carry a false sense of invulnerability. We have dwelt high in the clouds, in the presence of the Dream Giver himself, and we feel as if he may bear us right past the finish line, in a chariot like Elijah's.

But then reality bites. Sanctuary, we discover, was not a victory celebration but a battle preparation. We discover that the greatest challenges yet—human, natural, and supernatural—now rise up to blockade the port at journey's end.

And this time it's personal! Indeed, it will become very personal because the stakes are so high. The dream is about filling a need; writing a wrong; healing an illness on a large scale. The very forces responsible for that need, or that wrong, or that illness will be the forces we must now take on. And if defeating them were easy, someone would already have done it by now. David set his sites on the giant Goliath "because he has defied the armies of the living God" (1 Samuel 17:36). So it is with your own giants. They have defied the forces of good, and someone must bring them down.

They are tall, imposing, terrifying, and they come in a multitude of disguises. Never since the very outset of the dream has the task seemed so impossible; in fact, had we known about these giants, we would never have embarked. But here we are, by the grace of God, and it is not as if we are unarmed or unprepared. The Dream Giver himself has promised us two unvanquishable weapons: his presence and his power. In the very shadow of death, we will fear no evil, for he is with us. We haven't come this far to raise the white flag of surrender.

And so, fresh from the mountain, we stand with David and raise our sling. We take aim, fire—and the Battle for the Dream is joined. May God go with you!

> *Goliath was a shade over nine feet tall, which only added up to a bigger dent in the pavement. The bigger they come, the harder they fall.*
> —David Jeremiah

# QUOTES

*The great thing about facing giants is that in the end,
you discover you're a giant yourself.*

—UNKNOWN

*If you haven't got problems, you should get down on your knees
and ask, 'Lord, don't You trust me anymore?'"*

*"I am always crushed to hear people talk about the dreams
they used to have. Today they just plod along living day by day
doing whatever they've fallen into. Is that what God created
any of us for? Living without a passion and a dream
is equal to not living at all.*

—DREAMER IN PROVIDENCE, R.I.

*My pastor friend and his wife were broken-hearted—in a life
crisis. As I read them the first portion of* The Dream Giver, *they
wept together and settled into a new peace. Now they are soaring
toward their dream with a fresh wind beneath their wings.*

—DREAMER IN THE USA

## Instructions

Before viewing the video, read "The Purpose" and "The Promise" in this workbook session. Then watch the video and take notes on anything you want to remember or want to discuss with others.

After watching the video, go to "My Own Journey" to evaluate where you are in your own Dream Journey. If you are meeting with a group, and time allows, go through the questions in "My Group's Journey" for further discussion.

During the week, review "The Principles", "The Pitfalls", and "The Pattern", to learn even more about each stage of the Dream Journey.

## Video Notes:

_____

_____

_____

_____

_____

_____

_____

_____

_____

_____

_____

_____

_____

_____

## The Purpose

To discover the harsh reality of the great obstacles that must finally be toppled to achieve a dream; and to learn some attack strategies for facing them.

## The Promise

*David said to [Goliath] the Philistine, "You come against me with sword and spear and javelin, but I come against you in the name of the LORD Almighty, the God of the armies of Israel, whom you have defied . . . The whole world will know that there is a God in Israel. All those gathered here will know that it is not by sword or spear that the LORD saves; for the battle is the LORD's, and he will give all of you into our hands."* 1 SAMUEL 17:45, 46B, 47

*Do you not know that in a race all the runners run, but only one gets the prize? Run in such a way as to get the prize. Everyone who competes in the games goes into strict training. They do it to get a crown that will not last; but we do it to get a crown that will last forever. Therefore I do not run like a man running aimlessly; I do not fight like a man beating the air."* 1 CORINTHIANS 9:24-26

## The Principles

1. **Giants are hindrances that are real and must be faced.** They are powerful obstacles to the cure of the need we attempt to fill. Somehow they must be overcome.

   Some giants are "natural"; some are supernatural:
   *"For our struggle is not against flesh and blood, but against the rulers, against the authorities, against the powers of this dark world and against the spiritual forces of evil in the heavenly realms."* EPHESIANS 6:12

2. **Life's greatest climaxes and victories come in the Valley of Giants.** Because the Giants are tall, God gets more glory.

3. **God's greatest desire is for giant-killers.**
   *"For the eyes of the LORD range throughout the earth to strengthen those whose hearts are fully committed to him."* 2 CHRONICLES 16:9A

# The Pitfalls

Myths and misconceptions about the Valley of Giants

### 1. "Extreme courage: unnecessary. The giants will go down easily."

*Truth: This world's needs and wrongs become strongholds. Over time they strengthen and become more resistant to those who try to overcome them. There can be great danger, even physical danger, in taking on the giants that block your dream.*

### 2. "Extreme criticism: unlikely. People will respect the good I am trying to do."

*Truth: Criticism will come from unlikely the most surprising corners— from friends, associates, or even those we are trying to help.*

# The Pattern

There are many ways to take on the giants. Be discerning and creative.

### 1. Avoidance: If possible, simply stay away from the giant.

*"There was a plot afoot among the Gentiles and Jews, together with their leaders, to mistreat them and stone them. But they found out about it and fled to the Lycaonian cities of Lystra and Derbe and to the surrounding country."* ACTS 14:5-6

Paul and his companions avoid their opponents, and live to fight another day.

### 2. Alliance: Partner with others or even the giant himself.

*"Then Agrippa said to Paul, 'Do you think that in such a short time you can persuade me to be a Christian?'"* ACTS 26:28

Paul is tried by the king, and attempts to win him over.

### 3. Attack: Sometimes direct conflict is necessary.

*"While Paul was waiting for them in Athens, he was greatly distressed to see that the city was full of idols. So he reasoned in the synagogue with the Jews and the God-fearing Greeks, as well as in the marketplace day by day with those who happened to be there."* ACTS 17:16-17

## My Own Journey

This is your personal page. After you have completed the Valley of the Giants session, work through these questions in order to arm yourself against the Giants who oppose your dream.

1. The greatest Giant I have overcome in my life is: _____

_____.

2. While Giants are unpredictable, some of the greater obstacles I would expect to come up against in my own quest are: _____

_____.

3. For facing the Giants in the list above, here are some of the creative strategies that might be the most appropriate _____

_____.

4. On a scale of 1-10, 10 being the strongest, here is how I would grade my own present readiness for the Valley of Giants: _____

5. Here is what I believe I must do in my life to become stronger, wiser, and better prepared to face the Giants who will come forth to oppose me: _____

_____.

6. Therefore I make the following commitment(s) to act, beginning today, in accordance with the above:

Action(s): _____

When:_____

Who to tell: _____

Signature_____ Date _____

*(Write your commitment in this box, then sign and date it.)*

# My Group's Journey

If you set aside a time for group discussion during this session, use these questions to help you go deeper in your study of the Valley of Giants.

1. As you worked through this session, what was your greatest new insight about the obstacles known as Giants? Why?

2. Study the verses about David's words to the giant Goliath (1 Samuel 17:45-47). From what powerful idea does David draw his strength?

3. Even in faith, David had no guarantee of victory. Why do you think he was willing to take such a risk? How would your rate your own dreams in "life or death" value? Let various members respond.

4. What was David's true goal for the task of killing the giant? (verse 47)

5. Spend time in groups of two, discussing the Giants in your life and praying together for God to be glorified in your victory over them.

# The Land Of Promise

Astronaut Neil Armstrong tentatively slid his booted foot down the last rung of the ladder and became the first human being to touch the face of the moon. Can you imagine the emotions he must have felt?

How about the moment when Wilbur and Orville Wright discovered their homemade airplane was going to soar? Or the feeling of Joshua as he became the first Israelite to step onto the far bank of the Jordan River, in the land of Canaan?

There is nothing more exhilarating than the fulfillment of a dream—that moment when castles in the air become mansions on a hill. The "stuff of dreams," as Shakespeare called it, becomes real and visible. For days, months, perhaps decades you have pointed your whole life toward this moment. You've rehearsed it in your mind's eye countless times.

Now it's mission accomplished, and the world is different. But the greatest surprise is that so are you. You have upgraded the world in some way, and in the process, the dream has upgraded you. That's why your terminology is different; you speak now of needs and pain and injustices. The dream isn't really even about you anymore. It's about people you long to see healed and blessed. Something inside you shifted your motives from self to service.

That's why the whole dreamscape has changed. Your horizons are deeper and more distant. You see many more people beyond them—people with claims upon the heart of the Dream Giver.

It's easier than ever to see why the Dream Giver gave you this dream. Your personality, your gifts, and everything else fit into this work. In this Land of Promise you are like a nut that found its bolt.

And yet at the same time, you discover that this land is not your home. The assumption had always been that if you crossed over this line, you would be happy forever. But now things are different. That restlessness is already returning to your eye. Your friends catch you gazing toward the horizon, and you long to be on the move again; break through more walls; battle more giants.

Is this right? Yes it is, because the theater of life has more than one act. When the curtain comes down on the first one, the stage is illuminated even brighter for the second; and on and on. You discover that the dream that was entrusted to you is smaller than you thought; perhaps just a "training dream" compared to what lies ahead. The Dream Giver is saying, "Well done, good and faithful servant! You have been faithful with a few things; I will put you in charge of many things. Come and share your master's happiness!" (Matthew 25:21)

And that's what it's all about, isn't it? Sharing your master's happiness. You never knew happiness could be so deep, so joyful, as the meeting of human needs. You never knew your life could have so much impact, so much significance. But now, as one dream blossoms like a flower into a greater and more fragrant one, you're eager to see just how wide, how deep, and how vast is the abiding joy of the Dream Giver.

*Accomplishment will prove to be a journey, not a destination.*
—Dwight D. Eisenhower

# QUOTES

*If what you did yesterday seems big,*
*you haven't done anything today.*
—LOU HOLTZ

*My friend says she can sense a hidden dream in me bursting at*
*the seams to be released and realized! I have been drawn closer*
*to God than ever before. My dream includes helping people with*
*addictions gain freedom through the love of God.*

—A HELPER AND HEALER

*After a long time in the Wasteland, I'm beginning to see*
*a glimpse of my Promise Land and a few fellow Dreamers.*
*I recently created a new personal logo about two weeks*
*before getting this book for Christmas. My new logo*
*had a white feather in it, like The Dream Giver!*

—A DREAMER PUSHING FORWARD

*Let's try winning and see what it feels like.*
*If we don't like it,*
*we can go back to our traditions.*
—PAUL TSONGAS

## Instructions

Before viewing the video, read "The Purpose" and "The Promise" in this workbook session. Then watch the video and take notes on anything you want to remember or want to discuss with others.

After watching the video, go to "My Own Journey" to evaluate where you are in your own Dream Journey. If you are meeting with a group, and time allows, go through the questions in "My Group's Journey" for further discussion.

During the week, review "The Principles", "The Pitfalls", and "The Pattern", to learn even more about each stage of the Dream Journey.

## Video Notes:

_____

_____

_____

_____

_____

_____

_____

_____

_____

_____

_____

_____

_____

_____

_____

## The Purpose:

To explore the landscape that lies beyond the finish line of the dream, and to learn the truth about what comes afterward.

## The Promise:

*"So here I am today, eighty-five years old! . . . Now give me this hill country that the LORD promised me that day. You yourself heard then that the Anakites were there and their cities were large and fortified, but, the LORD helping me, I will drive them out just as he said."* JOSHUA 14:10C, 12

*"Brothers, I do not consider myself yet to have taken hold of it. But one thing I do: Forgetting what is behind and straining toward what is ahead, I press on toward the goal to win the prize for which God has called me heavenward in Christ Jesus."* PHILIPPIANS 3:13-14

## The Principles

1. **The Land of Promise is the exhilarating completion of the dream**
2. **The Land of Promise is the picture of the need having been met.**
3. **Meeting the need should be a skill that fits into your particular gift mix.**

## The Pitfalls:

1. **"The Land of Promise is the end line for me."**
   *Truth: It is the starting point for another dream.*
2. **"The Land of Promise will remain exciting."**
   *Truth: The thrill is temporary. We begin to look for other needs and other dreams beyond the present borders.*

# The Pattern

## 1. Empathize: Stay in touch with the need.

*"Jesus called his disciples to him and said, 'I have compassion for these people; they have already been with me three days and have nothing to eat. If I send them home hungry, they will collapse on the way, because some of them have come a long distance.'"* Mark 8:1c, 2,3

Jesus stayed among the hurting and felt their pain.

## 2. Effectiveness: Increase your productivity.

*"So the Twelve gathered all the disciples together and said, 'It would not be right for us to neglect the ministry of the word of God in order to wait on tables. Brothers, choose seven men from among you who are known to be full of the Spirit and wisdom. We will turn this responsibility over to them and will give our attention to prayer and the ministry of the word."* Acts 6:2-4

The early church organized itself to "work smarter."

## 3. Expansion: Push your borders outward for greater impact.

*"So after I have completed this task and have made sure that they have received this fruit, I will go to Spain and visit you on the way. I know that when I come to you, I will come in the full measure of the blessing of Christ."* Romans 15:28-29

Paul completed three dream journeys and to the very end he was pushing his borders outward, receiving the "full measure of the blessing of Christ."

## 4. Searching for need takes us deeper into the heart of the Dream Giver. The dreamer asks God to place within us His own heart and His own compassion.

*"Praise the LORD, O my soul, and forget not all his benefits—who forgives all your sins and heals all your diseases, who redeems your life from the pit and crowns you with love and compassion, who satisfies your desires with good things so that your youth is renewed like the eagle's."* Psalm 103:2-5

# My Own Journey

This is your private and personal page. After you have completed this final session of The Dream Giver, work through these questions in order to make your personal commitment to keep on until you cross into the Land of Promise.

1. I was most surprised to learn the following about the Land of Promise: _____.

2. Here is how I would evaluate or grade myself in the area of compassion toward the needs of others: _____

_____.

3. If I fulfilled my dream, the world might be different in the following way: _____.

4. If I fulfilled my dream, my own life and character would be different in the following way: _____.

5. Here is what I can be doing to help my heart be more like the Dream Giver's heart in relation to the needs of others: _____

_____.

---

6. Having completed The Dream Giver study course, reflected carefully and spent time with the Dream Giver himself, I feel that he is asking me to take the following action:

What: _____

When:_____

Who to tell: _____

Signature_____ Date _____

*(Write your commitment in this box, then sign and date it.)*

---

## My Group's Journey

If you set aside a time for group discussion during this session, use these questions to help you consider the material.

1. Describe the emotions you experience when you think of accomplishing your dream.

2. An elderly Joshua, having completed the dream of entering Canaan, asked for "one more mountain" (Joshua 14:10c, 12). What do you think motivated him to make this request of God?

3. Read Philippians 3:13-14. What aspects of Paul's attitude best typify a dream-chaser? How does his heavenly perspective make a difference?

4. How does it change us personally when God places within us His heart toward hurting people? How would it change your life right now?

5. In groups of two, close your session in prayer, encouraging one another to take practical and concrete steps toward following the dream God has given to each.

# THE
# DREAM
## GIVER

### ❧ LEADER'S GUIDE ❧

### Introduction: Getting the Most from The Dream Giver

Napoleon Bonaparte said, "A leader is a dealer in hope."

Napoleon had a dream for France and her citizens and he led the nation to hope in that dream. Your role as a leader, while perhaps on a smaller stage, is no less significant. Who knows? In your video seminar group could be a person God has called to change the course of a nation.

And you may be the one to give that person the hope they need to believe their dream is possible.

Welcome to *The Dream Giver Leader's Guide*! For the next eight or more weeks, you have the sacred calling to shepherd a group of dreamers from their Comfort Zones to their Land of Promise—or at least seeing them move in that direction. The purpose of this Leader's Guide is to help you lead them there; to equip you to become a "dealer in hope."

The practical information you are seeking first—"How, exactly, do I lead this video seminar?"—is under the heading below, "The Hands of the Leader." But please read through each of the following sections. Each one contributes something that will help you be an effective video seminar leader.

## The Hunger of the Leader

It has been said by many that you can't lead anyone further than you have gone yourself. The ideal person to lead The Dream Giver video seminar is a person who is hungry to realize his or her own dream—or perhaps is living it already.

During the course of this seminar, you, as the leader, must become a dream-seeker. Not just to play a role but to discover a reality! Begin today developing the mindset that your life is about to change. When those you are leading see your passion for living your dream, they will believe they can lead theirs as well.

## The Helper of the Leader

"But I'm not qualified," you might say. That's right—but who is? Even if you are currently living your dream, you are probably already formulating another. None of us has "arrived." But because God is the Dream Giver, He has committed His own Holy Spirit to be your helper (John 14:16, 26; 16:7). So depend on Him, beginning now. Ask for His help—His wisdom and discernment—on a daily basis throughout this course and beyond. God's dream is for you to lead this video seminar and He is committing His unlimited resources to make you successful.

## The Heart of the Leader

This seminar deals with weighty matters. Individuals, families, churches, communities—even nations—will be changed as the heart of man connects with the heart of God; as dreams become reality; as longings become lifestyles.

Jesus Christ told a story that illustrates how the condition of the heart determines the fruit that is born (Matthew 13:1-9). To that end, would you become especially attentive to your own heart and the hearts of those in your seminar group? You can do that three ways:

1. Pray daily for yourself: that God would empower you to be an instrument of His plan and purpose.

2. Pray consistently, by name, for those in your group: that they would be empowered to step out of their Comfort Zones and get on the road to their Land of Promise.

3. Be sensitive to what is happening in the lives of your group members: tend to their needs, encourage and nurture them as they break out of the cocoons where their dreams have been hibernating; share your own successes and failures with them.

## The Head of the Leader

Right behind heart-work comes homework. That's right—you've got lessons to prepare. Three steps will ensure you're ready week by week:

1. Watch the video lesson before each session. In fact, if you can watch it two or three times, all the better. (We always see and appreciate something new whenever we watch a favorite movie for the umpteenth time.) Take your own notes on the "Video Notes" page included with each session in the Workbook. In other words, immerse yourself in the message each week.

2. Work through the Workbook materials for each lesson before each session. Answer the questions, fill in the blanks, read the copy, make notes, jot down questions in the margin.

3. Gather corollary resource materials before each session. Scan the media for references to people fulfilling their dreams—stories you can use as illustrations, if needed, during class discussions. These stories are everywhere—if you look for them, you'll find them!

## The Habits of the Leader

Go where you want your group members to follow. If you will set high standards in the following areas, so will your seminar group:

1. Punctuality: begin and end each session on time, and keep the class moving ahead according to schedule.

2. Preparedness: have extra pens/pencils; have a couple of photocopied chapters of the session in case one or more forget their Workbooks; make sure the TV, VCR, and video tape are in working order. (Be ready to lead a class discussion in case of equipment failure—it can happen!).

3. Pleasantness: Your courtesy, positive attitude, and respect for others will set the tone for the group.

## The Hands of the Leader

General George S. Patton, Jr., said, "Never tell people how to do things. Tell them what to do and they will surprise you with their ingenuity."

As for the *What* of your job as seminar leader, it is two-fold: Show the video and moderate an energetic discussion of its principles.

As for the *How*, here are two outlines that work—outlines you are free to adjust to suit the unique needs and desires of your group:

*I. The One-Hour Format* (when The Dream Giver is used in a traditional Sunday School setting)

[*Note that each Workbook lesson consists of seven segments: Purpose, Promise, Principles, Pitfalls, Pattern, My Own Journey, and My Group's Journey. These segments are referenced below under the One-Hour and Hour-Plus formats.*]

*[2:00"]*   **A. Purpose:** Read the Purpose statement for the lesson. Use a brief illustration to expand its meaning (personal illustrations are always best).

*[2:00-4:00"]*   **B. Promise:** Call on class members to read the Scripture promises accompanying the lesson. On the basis of those promises, open the class in prayer asking God for enablement and freedom to understand and embrace the video message.

*[35:00-43:00"]*   **C. Show the Video:** Re-introduce Dr. Bruce Wilkinson each of the first few weeks to make sure late-comers know who the video speaker is. Encourage members to take notes on the blank "Video Notes" page included in each lesson in the Workbook.

*[2:00-4:00"]*   **D. Principles, Pitfalls, and Patterns.** Review quickly the Principles, Pitfalls, and Patterns covered in the video; simply repeating them will help confirm them.

*[10:00"]*   **E. My Own Journey.** Work through these questions, asking group members to respond with their answers. Encourage everyone to fill in this section of the Workbook as the discussion progresses.

*[Final moments]*   **F. Being a Dealer of Hope.** Encourage each member to use the Principles, Pitfalls, and Patterns points as a daily source of meditation and application during the week. Suggest that they keep

a daily journal of their thoughts, prayers, and dreams as they review the video message by using the Principles, Pitfalls, and Patterns points daily. Also encourage them to review and interact with the additional material provided under the "My Group's Journey" section. While there isn't enough time to include these points in the One-Hour Format, this section offers further stimulation and consideration of the points covered in the video.

**II. The Hour-Plus Format** (when The Dream Giver is used in a small group or Bible study setting that allows more time for discussion and interaction).

The primary difference with the *Hour-Plus Format* is adding the "My Group's Journey" section to the in-class discussion. After completing "E. My Own Journey" (above), lead the class in a consideration of the questions in the "My Group's Journey" section. Depending on the amount of time available, you can allocate additional time to reviewing "D. Principles, Pitfalls, and Patterns" as well.

The benefit of the Hour-Plus Format is primarily having more time available for group discussion, sharing of ideas, interaction between class members, and prayer time.

The Leader is free to adapt the general outlines above to his or her particular setting to ensure maximum effectiveness and the best use of time.

## The Hope of the Leader

Former president Harry Truman is well-remembered for this famous statement about leadership: "Leadership is the ability to get men to do what they don't want to do and like it."

In this series, Dr. Bruce Wilkinson will reveal something no one likes to do: leave his or her comfort zone. You may be the "dealer of hope" God uses to encourage someone in your group to step beyond their borders—to leave a long-standing comfort zone and pursue a long-standing dream.

May you serve your group well while depending on God's help, and see many pursue and embrace their dreams.

# Discovering Your Dream

## One-Hour Format

**I. INTRODUCE Session One: Discovering Your Dream** (Workbook, pages 7-8)  *[5:00"]*

• Welcome seminar attendees

• Introduce The Dream Giver video series
(see Workbook, pages 4-6)

• Introduce Dr. Bruce Wilkinson (see back cover)

> **Have you . . .**
>
> ❏ Watched the video?
>
> ❏ Read and completed the Workbook materials?
>
> ❏ Prepared the room?
>
> ❏ Prayed for this session and seminar members?

### A. PURPOSE of Session One  *[2:00"]*

• Introduce the purpose of Session One (page 11)

> • Stress that this Session's video message will summarize the entire seminar—the seven stages of the Dream Journey.

> • Offer an insight you gained through your personal viewing on Session One's video—something to watch for and note; a teaser for the class.

### B. PROMISE of Session One  *[2:00"]*

> • Read the two Scriptures on page 11.

> • Point out how Abraham "did not know where he was going," and the implications of such a venture (leaving one's comfort zone, fear of the unknown)

## II. WATCH the Video  *[29:00"]*

• Encourage the seminar members to take notes on the Video Notes page provided in the Workbook (page 10).

## III. REVIEW the Video  *[5:00"]*

• Principles

• Review the Seven Stages of the Dream Journey (p. 12).

• Ask how many people were able to identify which stage they are in (allow comments or discussion as time allows).

## IV. DISCUSS the Video Message  *[10:00"]*

• My Own Journey

• Go through the six points on page 13, encouraging seminar members to fill in the blanks and to share their answers with the group. Be sensitive to the personal nature of this information, perhaps sharing your own answers to get the discussion started.

• Commitment Block: ask each person to fill in the block at the bottom of page 13. If they are not ready to fill it in now, ask them to try to do it before Session Two begins.

• Stress the need for making a decision—purposing to break out of the Comfort Zone and begin pursuing their dream.

## V. APPLY the Video Message *[5:00"]*

• Give the following instructions to seminar members before leaving.

*A. Use the Principles* ("The Truth About Your Dream" and "The Seven Stages of the Dream Journey") as a daily meditation and source of inspiration for prayer.

*B. Incorporate the My Group's Journey questions* into your daily meditation and Bible Study

*C. Reread pages 7-8* at least once during the week.

*D. Read pages 15-16* to prepare for the next video Session.

*E. Dismiss the class with a prayer* of thanks for what He will do during the next seven weeks.

# Hour-Plus Format

• Complete steps I – III as outlined above in the One-Hour Format.

• Discussion under point III may be extended in light of the longer format.

• If needed, consider a 5-10 minute refreshment break after point III. before proceeding to the remainder of the Hour-Plus session.

## IV. DISCUSS the Video Message *[20:00"-45:00"]*

### A. My Own Journey

• See notes above for this section under the One-Hour format.

• Save question six, the Commitment block, until after the "My Group's Journey" exercise.

### B. My Group's Journey

• Take an extended time to work through the five questions on page 14.

• Following question five ("What commitments will you make . . . ?") return to question six on page 13. Encourage everyone to fill in this block. If some are not ready to do so now, encourage them to complete it before the next session.

• Complete step V as outlined above in the One-Hour Format.

# This Is Your Dream

## One-Hour Format

### I. INTRODUCE Session One: This Is Your Dream

(Workbook, pages 15-16) *[5:00"]*

• For the benefit of any who missed the first session, briefly re-introduce The Dream Giver video series (Workbook, pages 4-6) and the seminar teacher, Dr. Bruce Wilkinson (see back cover).

> **Have you . . .**
>
> ❏ Watched the video?
> ❏ Read and completed the Workbook materials?
> ❏ Prepared the room?
> ❏ Prayed for this session and seminar members?

#### A. Purpose of Session Two

• Introduce and summarize the purpose of Session Two (Workbook, page 19).

• Use an illustration of an individual who had a personal dream. For example, the famous "I Have a Dream" speech of Martin Luther King, Jr.

#### B. Promise of Session Two

• Assign the two scriptures on page 19 to two members and have them read the passages aloud.

• Ask for a show of hands: "How many people believe there is a powerful dream inside every person?"

### II. WATCH the Video *[33:00"]*

Encourage the seminar members to take notes on the Video Notes page provided in the Workbook (page 18).

### III. REVIEW the Video *[7:00"]*

Briefly . . .

#### A. Principles: review the three Principles (page 19)

#### B. Pitfalls: review the three Pitfalls (page 20)

#### C. Pattern: review the Four Stages in Discovering Your Dream (page 20)

### IV. DISCUSS the Video Message *[10:00"]*

• Go through the six points on page 21 ("My Own Journey"), encouraging seminar members to fill in the blanks and to share their answers with the group.

• Ask for a second show of hands: "How many now believe there is a dream inside every person?"

• Ask each person to fill in the box at the bottom of page 21 (Question 6). If time allows, ask one or two to share the commitment they recorded in the box.

## V. APPLY the Video Message *[5:00"]*

• Give the following instructions to seminar members before dismissing the group:

*A. Use the Principles, Pitfalls, and Pattern sections,* and the accompanying scriptures (pages 19-20) as a source for daily meditation and prayer during the week.

*B. Incorporate the My Group's Journey* questions into your daily meditation and Bible Study. (Encourage them to discuss those questions with family members or friends.)

*C. Reread pages 15-16* at least once during the coming week.

*D. Read pages 23-24* to prepare for the next video message.

*E. Ask if there is anyone who has experienced a "breakthrough"* in the first two weeks who would like to dismiss Session Two with a prayer of thanks to God.

# Hour-Plus Format

• Complete steps I – III as outlined above in the One-Hour Format.

• Discussion under point III. may be extended in light of the longer format.

• If needed, consider a 5-10 minute refreshment break after point III. before proceeding to the remainder of the Hour-Plus session.

## IV. DISCUSS the Video Message *[20:00"-45:00"]*

### A. My Own Journey

• Take as much time as necessary to help individuals embrace the idea that they have a dream inside them.

### B. My Group's Journey

• Suggest that the "hard work" (the personal journey questions) is complete. Now is a time to relax and dig in as a group to the questions on page 22. Start things off by sharing some of your own challenges in identifying your dream (Question 1).

• Complete step V as outlined above in the One-Hour Format.

# Your Comfort Zone

## One-Hour Format

### I. INTRODUCE Session Three: Your Comfort Zone

(Workbook, pages 23-24) *[5:00"]*

• Welcome seminar attendees

• Review the titles and purposes of the first two sessions:

• Session One: Discovering Your Dream—"seven key stages of the dream journey."

• Session Two: This Is Your Dream—"the nature of the dream and how to identify yours."

#### A. Purpose of Session Three

• Introduce the purpose of Session Three (Workbook, page 27)

• Ask someone to define "comfort zone." "What do you imagine Dr. Wilkinson is going to say about 'comfort zones' in this session's video?"

#### B. Promise

• Have two people look up the scriptures that go with this session (page 27).

• In both passages, what are people being asked to do? ("Leave their comfort zone!")

### II. WATCH the Video *[37:00"]*

• Encourage the seminar members to take notes on the Video Notes page provided in the Workbook (page 26).

### III. REVIEW the Video *[3:00"]*

As a brief review, call on people to talk through the four sets of points on pages 28.

#### A. Principles: touch on the two key principles (page 27)

#### B. Pitfalls: highlight the two misconceptions about the Comfort Zone (page 27)

#### C. Pattern: remind attendees why we stay in our Comfort Zone and how we break out of our Comfort Zone. (page 28)

> **Have you . . .**
>
> ❏ Watched the video?
>
> ❏ Read and completed the Workbook materials?
>
> ❏ Prepared the room?
>
> ❏ Prayed for this session and seminar members?

**IV. DISCUSS the Video Message** *[10:00"]*

• Work through the first five questions in "My Own Journey," asking for members to share their answers. Encourage everyone to fill in all the blanks.

• Ask each person to fill in the box at question six. Stress the importance of "driving a stake in the ground" each time they make one of these commitments.

**V. APPLY the Video Message** *[5:00"]*

• Give the following instructions to seminar members before dismissing the group:

*A. Use the Principles, Pitfalls, Pattern, and Breaking Through sections,* and the accompanying scriptures (pages 27-28), as a source for daily meditation and prayer during the week.

*B. Incorporate the My Group's Journey questions* into your daily meditation and Bible Study. (Encourage them to discuss those questions with family members or friends.)

*C. Reread pages 23-24* at least once during the coming week.

*D. Read pages 31-32* to prepare for the next video message.

*E. Ask if there is anyone who would like to "break out of their comfort zone"* and close the session in prayer.

# Hour-Plus Format

• Complete steps I – III as outlined above in the One-Hour Format.

• Discussion under point III. may be extended in light of the longer format.

• If needed, consider a 5-10 minute refreshment break after point III. before proceeding to the remainder of the Hour-Plus session.

**IV. DISCUSS the Video Message** *[20:00"-45:00"]*

*A. My Own Journey*

• Since you have more time, and if you have a chalk board or white board, put a 1-10 scale on the board and "graph" where the members are (questions two and four). Use this research to stimulate discussion: Numbers? Reasons? Implications?

• Have Scriptures ready as answers to question five.

*B. My Group's Journey*

• Be sure to take advantage of questions one, two, and five in your group setting.

• Complete step V as outlined above in the One-Hour Format.

# The Borderland

## One-Hour Format

### I. INTRODUCE Session Four: The Borderland

(Workbook, pages 31-32) *[5:00"]*

• Welcome seminar attendees

• Review the titles and purposes of the first three sessions. (Ask for volunteers to name the titles and purposes of each session.)

> **Have you . . .**
>
> ❑ Watched the video?
>
> ❑ Read and completed the Workbook materials?
>
> ❑ Prepared the room?
>
> ❑ Prayed for this session and seminar members?

#### A. Purpose of Session Four:

• Introduce the purpose of Session Four (page 27)

• "Quickly—let's name 10 things that intimidators do. We're going to discover that those same forces will come against you and your dream."

#### B. Promise

• Have two people look up the scriptures that go with this session (Workbook, p. 35).

• From the Numbers passage: "How many intimidators did it take to derail a nation of several million people?"

### II. WATCH the Video *[37:00"]*

• Encourage the seminar members to take notes on the Video Notes page provided in the Workbook (page 34).

### III. REVIEW the Video *[3:00"]*

Ask for three people to read and summarize each of the following points:

**A. Principles:** summarize the three key Borderland principles (page 35).

**B. Pitfalls:** what are two common misconceptions people have about their dream? (page 35)

**C. Border Bullies:** who are the Border Bullies? (page 35)

**D. Pattern:** what are three characteristics of Border Bullies? (page 36)

### IV. DISCUSS the Video Message *[10:00"]*

• Work through the first five questions in the "My Own Journey" section:

• Question 1: ask someone to share their experience.

• Question 2: ask for a show of hands on the most common "Bully."

• Question 3: Poll: where are most Border Bullies found? (Family? Work? Other?) Ask the same for Border Busters.

• Question 4: (Don't forget to include prayer unless it's mentioned by someone.)

• Question 5: Sensitive question: which category do most fall into?

• Question 6: Encourage each person to sign and date the commitment box.

## V. APPLY the Video Message *[5:00"]*

• Give the following instructions to seminar members before dismissing the group:

*A. Use the Principles, Pitfalls, Border Bullies, and Pattern sections,* and the accompanying scriptures (pages 27-28), as a source for daily meditation and prayer during the week.

*B. Incorporate the My Group's Journey questions* into your daily meditation and Bible Study. (Encourage them to discuss those questions with family members or friends.)

*C. Reread pages 31-32* at least once during the coming week.

*D. Read pages 39-40* to prepare for the next video message.

*E. Close with a prayer* of corporate confession for any time "we" have acted like a Border Bully in the lives of others, asking for courage to help others pursue their dream.

# Hour-Plus Format

• Complete steps I – III as outlined above in the One-Hour Format.

• Discussion under point III. may be extended in light of the longer format.

• If needed, consider a 5-10 minute refreshment break after point III. before proceeding to the remainder of the Hour-Plus session.

## IV. DISCUSS the Video Message *[20:00"-45:00"]*

### A. My Own Journey

• As members discuss these questions and fill in their Workbooks, be careful not to allow this discussion to become negative or "gossipy."

• Encourage attendees to use identifiers such as "a family member" or "a coworker" instead of names.

### B. My Group's Journey

• Discuss in your group the questions in this section.

• Complete step V as outlined above in the One-Hour Format.

# The Wasteland

## One-Hour Format

### I. INTRODUCE Session Five: The Wasteland

(Workbook, pages 39-40) *[5:00"]*

• Welcome seminar attendees

• Pass out half-sheets of paper containing two
columns: the titles of the first four sessions in one
column; the purpose statements in the second column
(in mixed order). As a review, have attendees draw
lines connecting the titles to the corresponding
purpose statements.

#### A. Purpose of Session Five

• Ask attendees for words that are synonymous with or adjectives
describing a "desert." Then introduce the purpose of Session Five
(Workbook, page 43).

#### B. Promise of Session Five

• Have two people look up and read the scriptures that go with this
session (Workbook, p. 43)

• From the James passage: "when" you encounter trials, not "if."

• What does Romans 8:28 imply about the possibility of "bad" things
happening?

### II. WATCH the Video *[36:00"]*

Encourage the seminar attendees to take notes on the Video Notes page
provided in the Workbook (page 42).

### III. REVIEW the Video *[4:00"]*

Review the message of Session Five by briefly highlighting the Principles and
Pitfalls (pages 43-44).

#### A. Principles

1. Assign the "D" words (page 44) to individuals; have them read the
quotes out loud one after another—with feeling! "Sound familiar?"

2. Ask for someone to recall the lessons from the video from the lives
of David and Joseph.

3. Fill in: "In the Wasteland, the is commensurate with the (pain, gain)

**B. Pitfalls**

> • Why does everyone think they will be the exception to the Wasteland? (What two misconceptions do all dreamers have?)

## IV. DISCUSS the Video Message *[10:00"]*

• My Own Journey

Attendees are "asking for trouble" by making this commitment. Begin this section with a brief prayer asking for wisdom and courage. Discuss and fill in each question, concluding with an invitation to sign the commitment box.

## V. APPLY the Video Message *[5:00"]*

• Give the following instructions to seminar members before dismissing the group:

> **A. Use the Principles and Pitfalls sections** (pages 43-44) as a source for daily meditation and prayer during the week. Encourage members to find scriptures as "antidotes" to the "D" words on page 44.

> **B. Incorporate the My Group's Journey questions** into your daily meditation and Bible Study. (Encourage members to discuss those questions with family members or friends.)

> **C. Reread pages 39-40** at least once during the coming week.

> **D. Read pages 47-48** to prepare for the next video message.

> **E. Close in prayer** using Deuteronomy 1:29-31 as a basis (especially verse 31).

# Hour-Plus Format

• Complete steps I – III as outlined above in the One-Hour Format.

• Discussion under point III. may be extended in light of the longer format.

• If needed, consider a 5-10 minute refreshment break after point III. before proceeding to the remainder of the discussion.

## IV. DISCUSS the Video Message *[20:00"-45:00"]*

> **A. My Own Journey**

> > • Take extra time in this segment to talk about the fears and hesitation attendees may have about venturing into the Wasteland.

> **B. My Group's Journey**

> > • These questions are a good opportunity for the power of "storytelling"— attendees' experiences in the Wasteland and God's provision.

• Complete step V as outlined above in the One-Hour Format.

# Sanctuary

## One-Hour Format

### I. INTRODUCE Session Six: Sanctuary

(Workbook, pages 47-48) *[5:00"]*

• Welcome seminar attendees

• Ask if there were any "Wasteland" experiences (Session Five) since the last meeting.

• Ask for a show of hands of those who signed the commitment box (page 45) either at the last meeting of during the week.

<table>
<tr><td>Have you . . .</td></tr>
<tr><td>❏ Watched the video?</td></tr>
<tr><td>❏ Read and completed the Workbook materials?</td></tr>
<tr><td>❏ Prepared the room?</td></tr>
<tr><td>❏ Prayed for this session and seminar members?</td></tr>
</table>

#### A. Purpose of Session Six

• Read Psalm 119:71 and correlate it with the purpose of Session Six (Workbook, page 51).

• What does the word "sanctuary" suggest about what precedes it?

#### B. Promise of Session Six

• Have two people read the two scriptures (page 51). "How is the idea of a sanctuary in the pursuit of a dream an evidence of God's grace?"

### II. WATCH the Video *[33:00"]*

Encourage the seminar attendees to take notes on the Video Notes page provided in the Workbook (page 50).

### III. REVIEW the Video *[5:00"]*

Review the message of Session Six by summarizing the points under Pitfalls and Pattern and Prinicples (pages 51-52).

#### A. Pitfalls

1. "What is the danger when we are consumed by our dream?"

2. "What do we learn by relinquishing our dream to the Dream Giver?"

#### B. Pattern and Principles

1. "What does Restoration imply?" (Wounding in the Wasteland.)

2. "What does Relationship imply?" (Dreams aren't accomplished without God.)

3. "What does Relinquishment imply?" (Our dreams do not belong to us in the end.)

## IV. DISCUSS the Video Message *[10:00"]*

• My Own Journey

These questions invade the spiritual domain of each dreamer. You don't *have* to be a Christian to pursue a dream, but if you're a Christian you have to pursue it while abiding in Christ (John 15). Watch for opportunities to explore the tension between "doing our own thing" and staying centered in Christ.

## V. APPLY the Video Message *[5:00"]*

• Give the following instructions to seminar members before dismissing the group:

*A. Use the Principles and Pitfalls sections* (pages 51-52) as a source for daily meditation and prayer during the week.

*B. Incorporate the My Group's Journey questions* into your daily meditation and Bible Study. (Encourage members to discuss those questions with family members or friends.)

*C. Reread pages 47-48* at least once during the coming week.

*D. Read pages 55-56* to prepare for the next video message.

*E. Read Psalm 131:1-3* as a prelude to prayer for a heart that longs to dwell at rest in God.

# Hour-Plus Format

• Complete steps I – III as outlined above in the One-Hour Format.

• Discussion under point III. may be extended in light of the longer format.

• If needed, consider a 5-10 minute refreshment break after point III. before proceeding to the remainder of the discussion.

## IV. DISCUSS the Video Message *[20:00"-45:00"]*

*A. My Own Journey*

See notes above on Section IV under "My Own Journey" (One-Hour Format). Extend this discussion to include more people and ideas as time allows.

*B. My Group's Journey*

Use the five questions as a catalyst for discussing the concept of Sanctuary—especially the various stages (see Principles). Vary the sizes of the groups (Questions 4 and 5) depending on the size of your overall group.

•Complete step V as outlined above in the One-Hour Format.

# Valley of the Giants

## One-Hour Format

### I. INTRODUCE Session Seven: Valley of the Giants

(Workbook, pages 55-56) *[3:00"]*

• Welcome seminar attendees

• Briefly recount the story of the Israelite spies who saw giants in the Promised Land and convinced Israel not to fulfill their dream (Numbers 13, especially verse 33).

| Have you . . . |
|---|
| ❏ Watched the video? |
| ❏ Read and completed the Workbook materials? |
| ❏ Prepared the room? |
| ❏ Prayed for this session and seminar members? |

#### A. Purpose of Session Seven.

• Introduce the purpose of Session Seven (page 59).

• Remind attendees that the Sanctuary (Session Six) was not a victory celebration but a battle preparation.

#### B. Promise of Session Seven

• Have two people read the scriptures on page 59.

• Why is it important to win battles and races that we cannot win in our own strength?

### II. WATCH the Video *[41:00"]*

Encourage the seminar attendees to take notes on the Video Notes page provided in the Workbook (page 58).

### III. REVIEW the Video *[3:00"]*

Review the message of Session Seven by summarizing the points under Principles and Pitfalls (pages 59-60).

#### A. Principles

1. "Denying the reality of giants won't make them go away.

2. "What are the three 'A's' of dealing with giants?

3. "The _____ they are, the _____ they fall—and the more _____ _____ God gets." (bigger, harder, glory)

#### B. Pitfalls

• Cite the two myths about giants and the truth that dispels them.

### IV. DISCUSS the Video Message *[10:00"]*

• My Own Journey

There are no new giants "under the sun." Everyone has encountered the giants of fear, finances, failure, frustration, and friendlessness. But don't forget legal and financial matters, time pressures, and other real life "giants." Make this a practical session focusing on practical solutions as well as identifying giants. Have attendees fill in the commitment box (Question Six), if not now then during the following week.

## V. APPLY the Video Message *[3:00"]*

• Give the following instructions to seminar members before dismissing the group:

*A. Use the Principles and Pitfalls sections* (pages 59-60) as a source for daily meditation and prayer during the week.

*B. Incorporate the My Group's Journey questions* into your daily meditation and Bible Study. (Encourage members to consider getting together with one or more fellow seminar attendees to work on this section.)

*C. Reread pages 55-56* at least once during the coming week.

*D. Read pages 63-64* to prepare for the next video message.

*E. Remind attendees of the spiritual armor of Ephesians 6:10-18.* Close with a prayer for faith to put on that armor and face the giants.

# Hour-Plus Format

• Complete steps I – III as outlined above in the One-Hour Format.

• Discussion under point III. may be extended in light of the longer format.

• If needed, consider a 5-10 minute refreshment break after point III. before proceeding to the remainder of the discussion.

## IV. DISCUSS the Video Message *[20:00"-45:00"]*

### A. My Own Journey

Use the suggestions for "My Own Journey" in the One-Hour Format (above), extending the discussion as time allows.

### B. My Group's Journey

The story of David and Goliath is well-known and becomes an easy backdrop for the questions in this section. As an expansion of Question Five, consider making a catalog of as many giants as the group can think of, arranged in categories (physical, logistical, spiritual, emotional, training, and others).

• Complete step V as outlined above in the One-Hour Format.

# The Land of Promise

## One-Hour Format

### I. INTRODUCE Session Eight: The Land of Promise

(Workbook, pages 63-64) *[5:00"]*

• Welcome seminar attendees

• Remind attendees that the last session of this video seminar is the first "session" of the rest of their lives— the launching pad to pursue and realize their dreams.

> **Have you . . .**
>
> ❏ Watched the video?
> ❏ Read and completed the Workbook materials?
> ❏ Prepared the room?
> ❏ Prayed for this session and seminar members?

#### A. Purpose of Session Eight

• Introduce the purpose of Session Eight (page 67)

• Every dream is the prelude to another dream; a further dimension of the great things God wants to do in you.

#### B. Promise of Session Eight

• Have two people read the scriptures on page 67.

• Caleb was 85 when he received his inheritance, Paul was a rabbinic scholar. It's never too late to pursue and realize your dream!

### II. WATCH the Video *[36:00"]*

Encourage the seminar attendees to take notes on the Video Notes page provided in the Workbook (page 66).

### III. REVIEW the Video *[4:00"]*

Review the message of Session Eight by summarizing the points under Principles and Pitfalls (pages 67-68).

#### A. Principles

1. Remember: dreams are about meeting human needs. Don't lose sight of the goal!

2. Work smarter as well as harder.

3. Don't be satisfied with just achieving "Stage One" of your dream.

#### B. Pitfalls

1. Truth: the Epilogue for one dream becomes the Prologue for another.

2. Truth: as soon as you get to Stage Seven, you find yourself in another Comfort Zone out of which you must break. The cycle begins again.

## IV. DISCUSS the Video Message *[10:00"]*

• My Own Journey

Use this final discussion session for personal reflections and testimonies on what attendees have learned. Use the commitment box (Question Six) to record plans for the future.

## V. APPLY the Video Message *[5:00"]*

• Give the following instructions to seminar members before dismissing the group:

*A. Use the Principles and Pitfalls sections* (pages 67-68) as a source for daily meditation and prayer during the week.

*B. Incorporate the My Group's Journey* questions into your daily meditation and Bible Study. (Encourage members to consider getting together with one or more fellow seminar attendees to work on this section.)

*C. Reread pages 63-64* at least once during the coming week.

*D. Allow different members to offer prayers of thanks* to God for what has been learned. Close in prayer—that the Dream Giver would allow every dream to be realized.

# Hour-Plus Format

• Complete steps I – III as outlined above in the One-Hour Format.

• Discussion under point III. may be extended in light of the longer format.

• If needed, consider a 5-10 minute refreshment break after point III. before proceeding to the remainder of the discussion.

## IV. DISCUSS the Video Message *[20:00"-45:00"]*

*A. My Own Journey*

Use this final discussion session for personal reflections and testimonies on what attendees have learned as they fill in the questions. Use the commitment box (Question Six) to record plans for the future.

*B. My Group's Journey*

Use insights from the lives of Joshua and Paul (Questions Two and Three) to gain insight into being a dream-chaser. As an expansion of Question Five, have the group spend time sharing how their lives are different after taking this video seminar course, and what they plan to do to pursue their dream.

• Complete step V as outlined above in the One-Hour Format.

## Dream Giver Resources

Live your dream. That is the key message from #1 *New York Times* bestselling author Bruce Wilkinson. *The Dream Giver* is a journey from the ordinary to the extraordinary. This teaching, from a live seminar taught by the author, invites you to follow your heart and find your destiny in an inspired Life Dream that is uniquely yours.

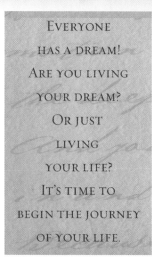

EVERYONE HAS A DREAM! ARE YOU LIVING YOUR DREAM? OR JUST LIVING YOUR LIFE? IT'S TIME TO BEGIN THE JOURNEY OF YOUR LIFE.

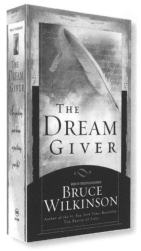

This visual adaptation of the best-selling book is an 8-part series, ideal for group or individual study. Each session is 30-40 minutes in length.

VHS – *2 VHS tapes*

Also included as a special feature on the DVD and VHS set, hear interviews with Rick Warren, John Tesh, Robert Schuller, George Forman, Kirk Cameron, and Delilah.

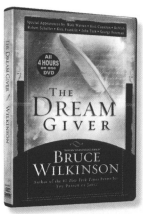

DVD – *1 DVD*

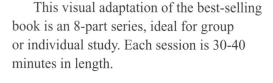

**www.brucewilkinson.com**

Workbook with
Leader's Guide
*(96 pp)*

Cassette – *4 cassettes*

CD – *4 CDs*

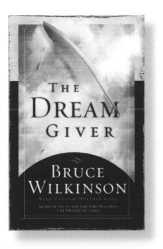

Also available, the original book:
The Dream Giver Book *(160 pp)*

The Dream Giver Audio Book
*(read by the author)*

## More Resources from Bruce and Darlene Marie Wilkinson

Now experience the entire message as never before!

You may have already read the best-selling books by Bruce and Darlene Marie Wilkinson . . . *The Prayer of Jabez, The Prayer of Jabez for Women, Secrets of the Vine,* and more. As life-altering as they may be, the books simply cannot compare with the companion video seminars!

These DVD, VHS and Audio Seminars take the spiritual truths in the books to a far deeper level, creating an entire learning experience designed to guide you through spiritiual breakthroughs that will make incredible positive changes in your life!

Ideal for Sunday School, small groups and personal study, each user-friendly multimedia series builds on the previous ones to lead you into an ever-deeper understanding of scriptural truths that draw you closer to God and His will for your life.

## Secrets of the Vine

The adventure of living the abundant life is the focus of the teaching on the *Secrets of the Vine*. This study on the words of Jesus in John 15 will help you understand that God longs to see your basket of fruit filled to overflowing!

## The Prayer of Jabez

Are you ready to experience the blessings God longs to give each of us? Join Bruce Wilkinson in looking at 1 Chronicles 4:10 to discover how the remarkable prayer of a little-known Bible hero can release God's favor, power, and protection.

## The Prayer of Jabez for Women

Take a journey with author and speaker Darlene Marie Wilkinson as she explores the Prayer of Jabez from a uniquely feminine perspective. Personal stories from her life and the lives of others will reveal new insights into God's word.

## A Life God Rewards

In this video series you're going to discover that Jesus revealed a direct link between what you do today and what you will experience after you die. Bruce Wilkinson shows you what Jesus said about God's plan to reward you in eternity for what you do for Him today.

## The Vision of the Leader

Do you feel it? Something stirring deep inside you? It's a thing that makes your heart surge—a thing of hope and anticipation. Bruce Wilkinson explores how to birth the Vision within you, to come to maturity, and to carry to heights never dreamed possible.

---

*Available in:*

- DVD Video Series
- VHS Video Series
- Audio CD Series
- Audio Cassette Series
- Course Workbooks
- Leader's Guides

## www.globalvisionresources.com